Grace Be Grace Do
2025 Edition

ISBN 978-1-06706-525-6

Author : Peter Koren
Publisher : GLOWING LIGHT LTD
Auckland New Zealand
Paperback
Copyright © August 2012

Grace Be Grace Do 1
GLOWING LIGHT LTD 2
Foreword 3
Introduction 5
   CHAPTER 1 11
   CHAPTER 2 39
   CHAPTER 3 51
   CHAPTER 4 73
   CHAPTER 5 91
   CHAPTER 6 109
   CHAPTER 7 129
   CHAPTER 8 167
   CHAPTER 9 191
   Transforming Empowering Resurrection Life
Scriptures: 197
Grace Be Grace Do images attribution:- 201

*All rights reserved worldwide.
No part of this publication may be replicated,
redistributed, or given away in any form without
the prior written consent of the author/publisher or
the terms relayed to you herein.*

*Grace Be Grace Do
2025 Version*

Published by GLOWING LIGHT LTD

Has a new cover, a new chapter and an added illustration. This is still a very relevant message for 2025. With so much happening in this world following 2020, believers need the ever increasing abundance of grace; as sin abounds grace abounds evermore.

Foreword

Peter Koren has been through the trials and tribulations that life and the enemy will often bring against God's children.

In these pages he has shared with you how he has, with the help of a loving Father, the Holy Spirit, and Jesus found victory.

May you be inspired to grab hold of the hem of His garment and claim the victory also.

In His Amazing Love,

Rev. Darrick E. DeBoard, Sr, CCC
Founder and President His Spirit International

Peter's book is filled with encouragement and his experiences with the Lord will help you in your journey to go higher into His presence.

Peter uplifts spirits and moves readers in the direction of the Lord.
Peter is a blessing to many.

Pam Barranco
Seeing Through the Eyes of God International.

Introduction

This book is written to encourage believers that are struggling with issues and their faith to overcome; to see that there is a way to change and how to be in position for breakthrough.

Achilles was a great warrior, but he had the weakness in the heel, the enemy will always aim for and fire arrows into our weakness to bring us down, he wants to knock us off our footing and bring us down where he can dominate us. We are destined to be a great warrior and achieve our individual greatness, unlike Achilles we need to be cleansed and revived in the river of life.

We have access to the empowering from the Kingdom of God and the strength that He has provided for our breakthrough, out of the old ways and into the new.

We are in the time of acceleration and the season of breakthrough.
It is time for the years of endless struggle to be overtaken by the grace of God. Our weakness will become His strength in the new season of walking into who we really are in Christ.

The resources of Heaven are at our request to fulfill the quest.

Expect the suddenlies of God, expect radical change when the day of turnaround dawns and shines through and burns away our past by the brightness of Gods Glory filling our lives.

Yes there still will be those times where growth occurs through processes and seasons, this is part of the eternal law of seed and harvest. When you plant a seed in the right conditions it will flourish and produce much life.

God sends His word to deliver us and bring restoration which empowers us to walk out of where we have been to where He sees us going in life.
God reveals Dreams of our future and who He sees we can be and what we can do in this life.

Years of deeply rooted, behavioural patterns and generational traits are embedded into our souls, like tracks layered and imprinted into our minds, memories and emotions are triggered by the storms of life. This is what the enemy of our souls uses to influence us and keep us from becoming the person God intended us to be.
The love and the power of God reaches deep and long and wide and far into our beings to deliver us from the power of the past, to make us into a new creation man and woman of God. His Grace will cover our iniquities and weaknesses to be who He made us to be and will empower us to do what we were made to do.

He who began a good work will complete it.
He is the author and finisher of our faith.
Jesus is the Alpha and the Omega.
He knows our beginning and where we will be.
God the Father by the Holy Spirit strengthens us to battle through the journey to our promised land.

Growing up can be a struggle for each of us in individual ways and we need to know how to rise above and have a strategy to win; which is individual for each of us as we appropriate change.

Just like Jacob he struggled and wrestled with the angel of God all night asking for a blessing.
Genesis 32:24
24 Then Jacob was left alone; and a Man wrestled with him until the breaking of day.

Some battles I win.
Some battles are ongoing and sometimes I may make one step forward and then find myself driven two steps back.
Join me in what I have discovered to help me rise above.
Contrary to where I am at, I have come to know God's never ending love that lifts me higher and have gained His strength to carry on.

The opening chapters introduce the position of victory that we have been freely given in Christ.

The remaining chapters will help us to walk it out with some valuable *how to go about it* guidance and then to cap it off, where faith is headed, arise and shine the Glory of God is here.
Find the peace and love of God on the way, as you get to know Him better that is where it is at, the True Light is shining.

Battles will come and battles will go.
There is a way out and upward.
He knows the outcome and where we are at in the now.
That doesn't stop Him because He is the God of love and hope for our future.
The important thing is how we finish.

I believe that the revelations and strategies revealed in this book will encourage the reader that there is a way to get off the out of control and the spinning faster, mad world, merry go round.

You will be challenged to go higher and not accept defeat as what was once impossible, becomes your possibility in Him.
Grace to be and Grace to do is what it is all about.

Read on into your promised victory.
The Journey is well worth it and you will be eternally grateful.

Isaiah 40:27 – 31.
27 Why do you say, O Jacob,
And speak, O Israel:
"My way is hidden from the Lord,
And my just claim is passed over by my God"?
28 Have you not known?
Have you not heard?
The everlasting God, the Lord,
The Creator of the ends of the earth,
Neither faints nor is weary.
His understanding is unsearchable.
29 He gives power to the weak,
And to those who have no might He increases strength.
30 Even the youths shall faint and be weary,
And the young men shall utterly fall,
31 But those who wait on the Lord
Shall renew their strength;
They shall mount up with wings like eagles,
They shall run and not be weary,
They shall walk and not faint.

CHAPTER 1

Resurrection Life

"He's been resurrected from the dead"
it is a *"he has come back from the dead"*
expression.
Coming back to life when he was down and out of the scene.
Like a has-been star that makes a comeback and surprises everybody, when he makes the comeback of his career and finds a new zing and charisma with a fresh lease of life.

Let's take an extreme example from the Word of God, where a man called Lazarus actually died and was then resurrected from the dead by the ministry of Jesus.
John 11:1- 44 is the following versus studied, you may read this first.

Beginning in *John 11:3* they inform Jesus about His friend Lazarus -
"he whom you love is sick"
In this life there is much sickness and disease - that is also known as infirmities and these are weaknesses that we are prone to and overtake us in this world, Jesus still loves us when we are afflicted.

John 11:4 Jesus declares with complete faith
"this sickness is not unto death".

Sickness does not have to end up in death - when death overshadows us, we can receive His promise of healing and the invigorating life which will set us free, put yourself in receive mode.
Sickness is only a symptom of a decaying factor of a world separated from Gods restorative energy and life force, this energy is alive and will surge through the building blocks of life, the cells of our human frame.

Jesus boldly states with Authority *"The Son of God is glorified through the sickness."* - now without Jesus we are a lost cause and so, when He comes onto the scene, there is life, healing, deliverance and freedom, as His Glory is the saving life for mankind.
In our trials in this life, the Glory of God is revealed when we receive breakthrough and have a testimony of His goodness.

John 11:6 Jesus stayed two more days in the place where He was - symbolic of His position in Heaven, after His resurrection, seated at the right hand of the Father, He is the Head of the Church, the Body of believers and symbolic of about 2000 years before He returns.
We won't debate exact times and seasons this is not the point of this book, it is an observation of a symbolic type,
a day being like a thousand years to God - it has meaning and represents some mechanism of Gods timetable and where His church is positioned.

John 11:9 Jesus declares a truth
"I am the Light of the World"
Darkness hides the truth and covers the true condition, when the Light shines it reveals the condition, we need the Light of the World to come to show the condition of this world and reveal the truth that will set us free.

John 11:14 Jesus spells it out plainly on our level
"Lazarus is dead".
Whoops! Oh dear! He is dead Jesus, what are we going to do now Jesus? Thomas suggests going to Jerusalem, getting hammered by persecution for being a follower of Christ and dying as well.
However, Jesus is not phased by the appearance of doom and the circumstances; He sees what His Father in Heaven is doing and proceeds with the infallible plan of God in this dire situation.

We are dead figuratively as well and things look very dire for us, until He resurrects us back to life.
Now Lazarus was 4 days in the tomb - symbolic of 4000 years until Jesus came to earth from the beginning of mankind as described in Genesis.
Mankind since the fall (when Adam and Eve first sinned in the Garden of Eden) is dead in the tomb, as good as dead, without hope in this world until Jesus came to declare freedom and give us hope for a new life.

Romans 5:12-14
12 Therefore, just as through one man sin entered the world, and death through sin, and thus death spread to all men, because all sinned—
13 (For until the law sin was in the world, but sin is not imputed when there is no law.
14 Nevertheless death reigned from Adam to Moses, even over those who had not sinned according to the likeness of the transgression of Adam, who is a type of Him who was to come.

Next Jesus gets very bold in the face of a very dire case of death.
John 11:25
Jesus said to her, "I am the resurrection and the life. He who believes in Me, though he may die, he shall live.

What a bold statement in the face of death! **"I AM the Resurrection and the LIFE".** How can anyone say that when you can clearly see the exact opposite?
Jesus is the complete answer for the death of mankind due to sin and He came to demonstrate His intentions to save us from death.
John 11:26 Jesus says *"whoever lives and believes in Me will never die".*

We are brought out of the sentence of death imposed upon us from birth, into His eternal life as a new revived man.

Romans 5:17
17 For if by the one man's offense death reigned through the one, much more those who receive abundance of grace and of the gift of righteousness will reign in life through the One, Jesus Christ.

Now! Today! We can receive the abundance of living by His grace which is unearned by our performance and we are placed in a new position of being righteous through faith in Jesus, the sentence of death and the sickness that sin brings will no longer hold us down. That's how we can rule and reign in Christ Jesus, from the new position given to us and this is by grace and we will see that the abundance of grace offers us so much more in the ability to rule and reign.

John 11:35
Jesus wept.
His compassion for the suffering of mankind is evident.
The love of God is never ending.
John 11:39 Jesus commands *"take away the stone from the Tomb".*
Do you ever feel like you are in a place of entombment, locked into a dark confined dungeon?

A stone is a weight placed over an entry point and the exit - you can't get out and nobody can get in to help you.

We need an entry point and an exit point to be able to connect with the life energy of Heaven that really is liberating in the realm of the spirit, we are spiritual beings and we need to able to have this freedom to really live fully and exit the place of death.
There is a stench of death in the air - without Jesus we are left to decay by the shadow of death, which will take its natural course of degeneration also in our mortal bodies.

We don't have to accept the onslaught of death and sickness, which like in Lazarus's case brought death before his time to complete his journey on earth. God has so much for us to experience and understand in this part of the journey in our mortal bodies, we can come to know Him and be His friend like Lazarus and his sisters walking with Him and talking with Him in this time-line that we have been given on earth.

John 11:40 Jesus declares *"if you believe you will see the glory of God".*
Only believe - that is our part to receive the goodness of God.
John 11:43 *He cried in a loud voice*

When Jesus comes to sort out a problem, He means business and He commands the situation as the Lion of Judah, the King of kings and the Lord of lords, the job will be done guaranteed and He is our example to follow.

Jesus cried out *"Lazarus come forth"*
He calls us out of death and says to us *"come forth"* and come alive in Me. When you hear Him calling out to you *"come forth"* He means business and He is about getting you sorted in Life.

John 11:44 Jesus commands *"loose him from the grave clothes"*.
Our old garments of death that restrain us and keep us contained in a place of death will be removed.

Zechariah 3:1-5
1 Then he showed me Joshua the high priest standing before the Angel of the Lord, and Satan standing at his right hand to oppose him.
2 And the Lord said to Satan, "The Lord rebuke you, Satan! The Lord who has chosen Jerusalem rebuke you!
Is this not a brand plucked from the fire?"
3 Now Joshua was clothed with filthy garments, and was standing before the Angel.
4 Then He answered and spoke to those who stood before Him, saying, "Take away the filthy garments from him." And to him He said, "See, I have removed your iniquity from you, and I will clothe you with rich robes."
5 And I said, "Let them put a clean turban on his head."
So they put a clean turban on his head, and they put the clothes on him. And the Angel of the Lord stood by.

Joshua the High priest was given new clothes and a turban was placed on his head. Joshua was a chosen minister of God and he was wearing filthy clothes. God is in the business of rebuking the enemy of mankind and His intention is to remove the filth from us that weighs us down.

God deals with the issue of sin in our life and gives us a brand new covering on our heads for our thinking, which was stinking.
Notice what Satan does, he is standing at his right hand and the right hand symbolizes ability and what is produced and he opposes him.

Old grave clothes keep us bound and are quite grubby and we look like death warmed up until we are given a new lease of life.
New clothes will fit us well, with the robes of Righteousness that make us shine and provide us with the warm coat of Gods Glory.
It can be a brand new day for us when we receive brand new clothes from Heaven and our thinking has been renewed, this has all been provided when we enter into His Kingdom.

Our part is to yield to the process in the journey of development bringing change, as we grow up into His New Life and divine nature, learning His ways to put on brand new clothes in the glory.

However, we can also believe for the suddenlies of breakthrough as well, angels come to assist us and usher in a breakthrough moment that will remove the old weights and the worn out and grubby clothes of yesterday. Maybe we need relief from a long oppressive battle of the wars and negative forces of this world that oppose us, hammering our mind, emotions and bodies, like what Satan does, he opposes, so that is the source of attack.
Our old restrictive garments need to be replaced and we may receive new mantles and giftings that will take us into a whole new level in His Kingdom.

Philippians 3:9-14
9 and be found in Him, not having my own righteousness, which is from the law, but that which is through faith in Christ, the righteousness which is from God by faith;
10 that I may know Him and the power of His resurrection, and the fellowship of His sufferings, being conformed to His death,
11 if, by any means, I may attain to the resurrection from the dead.
12 Not that I have already attained, or am already perfected; but I press on, that I may lay hold of that for which Christ Jesus has also laid hold of me.
13 Brethren, I do not count myself to have apprehended; but one thing I do, forgetting those things which are behind and reaching forward to those things which are ahead,
14 I press toward the goal for the prize of the upward call of God in Christ Jesus.

Paul is saying that we can be found in Him, in Jesus who is the Resurrection and the Life and that means that it is a position given to us of righteousness that is not our own, you see we are found in Him which is His Righteousness and this is the freedom, we were lost and now we are found.

Then we move on and really get to know Him, there is knowledge about the power of His Resurrection. You know! What is the resurrection and the life of God really offering us?

It is an act of determination to take hold of what is available to us as believers, this means the weights of the past and the wounds inflicted upon us can no longer hold us back, we can adjust our vision and align our thinking with Heaven and move on to our God given destiny.

There is a goal and a prize when we go through the process of change with the power of His Resurrection Life and we fix our eyes on Jesus, the Overseer of our souls and provider of our true place of living.

So what would being conformed to His death be about? Why would you have to go the way of death if you are coming alive out of a death? It is like saying to Lazarus, Jesus just raised you from the dead, but now God wants to kill you and you gotta go back to the tomb and die again.

No, God's will is not for us to go back to our previous place of bondage, there is another way to go and someone went there before us and took the very power of death upon Himself.

Rom 4:16-25
16 Therefore it is of faith that it might be according to grace, so that the promise might be sure to all the seed, not only to those who are of the law, but also to those who are of the faith of Abraham, who is the father of us all
17 (as it is written, "I have made you a father of many nations") in the presence of Him whom he believed—God, who gives life to the dead and calls those things which do not exist as though they did;
18 who, contrary to hope, in hope believed, so that he became the father of many nations, according to what was spoken, "So shall your descendants be."
19 And not being weak in faith, he did not consider his own body, already dead (since he was about a hundred years old), and the deadness of Sarah's womb.
20 He did not waver at the promise of God through unbelief, but was strengthened in faith, giving glory to God,
21 and being fully convinced that what He had promised He was also able to perform.
22 And therefore "it was accounted to him for righteousness."
23 Now it was not written for his sake alone that it was imputed to him,

24 but also for us. It shall be imputed to us who believe in Him who raised up Jesus our Lord from the dead,
25 who was delivered up because of our offenses, and was raised because of our justification.

OK what is the position here? - Abraham faced the fact that his body was as good as dead. What is God offering here? God gives life to the dead - calls things that are not as though they are.

Abraham was about 100 years old and he has the promise of God *"your descendants"*, Sarah his wife is about the same age, things are looking desperate, God waited too long once again, but not for a miracle.

That seems to be the way God moves, by miracles, the Glory goes to Him and He is acting contrary and beyond the limitations of this world.

So don't give up in your circumstances when things look totally lost, take heart from this example where Abraham and Sarah were strengthened in faith, to the point that they believed God would perform what He had promised them.

You see that they faced the fact that their body was as good as dead, yes there are facts and they tell us what the situation is, they give us a report that is the picture of the circumstances that we face in life.

When all of the odds are stacked against us, we could be written off and left for dead. God has a way of giving life to the dead and calling things that are not as though they are. God looks at the facts and He sees and knows without a doubt His promise is truth, His power and His future and the truth of how things really are through the perspective from above, looking at the circumstances by faith is a whole new world.

Now it is going to take time for us to catch on isn't it? Especially if we are used to being down and out and thinking with no hope, we are going to need to put on a whole new mindset and begin to see things in the light of a new perspective - which is faith.

Abraham just like us had to go through the limits of his natural strength and ability and reached the end of the line, as the death in his body kicked in and ultimately, old age brings decline; and at 100 years old he could not physically conceive and Sarah was the same, the womb was physically past it, good as dead. They had to rely completely on the power of God to conceive, it is the life of God based on His promise that enabled them to have a miracle child.
Do you see the illustration for us?

We cannot conceive in our own ability the promises of God, we need to come to the end of ourselves and by faith receive life from God.

Just like Lazarus received, when Jesus came with His Resurrection and the Life, he was enabled, miraculously to be raised up to a whole new life in God.

The Son of God is glorified as there was no possible way that Lazarus or anybody else made him live, as it is God who gives life to the dead.
We need to stop striving and trying to make it happen, as it cant happen until we enter into the promise of God for our life and be strengthened in faith that God will perform what He has promised us.

We will never be able to conceive the promise and plan for our lives in our own natural ability that is flawed by the nature of death, if we do try we will produce an Ishmael, a flesh product that is not from above, that is bound by the laws that operate on our level, which is headed for decay, as the Resurrection Life is not accessed by an act of the flesh.

Abraham could either be known as the father of Ishmael, which he achieved in his own natural abilities, or be known as someone who conceived the promised child, as the father of faith in what God had promised and in the strength he received from God to perform. This leads us to the powerful overcoming truths on this subject from *Romans 8*, the chapter of total victory and a new principle of life at work in us who believe.

Rom 8:10-14
10 And if Christ is in you, the body is dead because of sin, but the Spirit is life because of righteousness.
11 But if the Spirit of Him who raised Jesus from the dead dwells in you, He who raised Christ from the dead will also give life to your mortal bodies through His Spirit who dwells in you.
12 Therefore, brethren, we are debtors—not to the flesh, to live according to the flesh.
13 For if you live according to the flesh you will die; but if by the Spirit you put to death the deeds of the body, you will live.
14 For as many as are led by the Spirit of God, these are sons of God.

What happens to our bodies if we are mortal creatures of death?
We die.
However, when the Spirit of Him who raised Jesus from the dead lives in us and gives life to our mortal body.
We Live.

There is life available for us who believe and it is Resurrection Life - it has the same power that raised Jesus from the dead and it is for here and now, living right here in this body on earth that you presently exist in, when all about you is images of death and disease, the life of God is right there, ready to plug in and radically change your whole person from the inside to the external cells of your body, now that is radical faith.

We are now debtors and we owe something in the exchange of Heaven, as Jesus paid the price of dying on our behalf for our sins and gave us the Spirit of life.

The principle of receiving the resurrection life to change us radically has a requirement; that in order for there to be a resurrection there must first of all be a death.

Jesus went before us and He died on the cross in our place and took the sins of the whole world upon Himself, in the sacrifice of the ages that is able to set all of mankind free. Our part is to identify with this death, why?

If the natural still remains, it will produce death or conceive of its nature and that is a sin nature of death.

That is our debt and the exchange has already been done for us and the credit is the resurrection life He gave us, so in order to complete the transaction we need to place the body of sin where it belongs in His death on the cross, where it no longer rules our life towards sin and death.

So we enter in at the point of the cross and then as the stone is rolled away, we come back out changed with the resurrection life, this is the process that we enter into.

If we continue to live our life in the flesh we will die - so if we go our own way and rule our life without God, we will not enter into His resurrection life but remain in death, decaying in the grave clothes that are filthy and keep us bound up in the habits of our past.

How then can we do this new life that God has offered? It is by the Spirit that we put to death the deeds of the body - we live from an empowering that God deposited into Jesus when He was raised up again from the dead, the life of God enters into our spirit that has been made alive again.

We have been switched on after being dead, when we enter into the exchange of our lives in the life giving process.
How do we enter into the process of change? Those who are led by the Spirit are Sons of God, this process will go on as a life style choice, as we mature and develop a sensitivity to His Spirit that takes us where we are at and shows us the way to go higher.

Gal 2:20, 21
20 I have been crucified with Christ; it is no longer I who live, but Christ lives in me; and the life which I now live in the flesh I live by faith in the Son of God, who loved me and gave Himself for me.
21 I do not set aside the grace of God; for if righteousness comes through the law, then Christ died in vain."

Now that is faith, that we have already been crucified with Him, our old nature has been dealt with on the cross, now we need to activate this place of exchange by identifying with the cross where our sinful nature was crucified with Christ.

He took our sins upon Himself as an innocent and perfect sacrifice on our behalf and now it is up to us to go there with our faults and weaknesses by faith, we are wearing our old clothes and we are filthy, in this place of exchange God is there to remove them from us and place His garments on us, so we put righteousness on and receive the new life within of radical change.

The truth is that we are the Righteousness of God and the old has gone and this is our position in Christ as we now have access and therefore, can on a daily basis appropriate what rightly belongs to us as believers.

It is not the act of salvation over and over; it is growing up into Him and becoming mature Sons of God who follow Him.
When we struggle with sins and are the living dead and have a nature that stinks, we can put our trust in the resurrection life of Jesus that will call us forth from the ways of death to a new life, freeing us from the grave clothes that restrict us.

It is good to believe that Jesus saved us and died for our sins and we have his forgiveness, but we need to also take hold of the miracle working power of His resurrection life that has raised us up out of sinful bondage.

We need to see that Jesus really did come to set us free and we have ongoing growth towards maturity. It's a life choice that we can partake of and salvation is the first point of entry that gains us the right to receive the new life that we walk into.

Here is a matter of fact and historical evidence, that Jesus went to the cross and died for our sins, but He did not stay there.
He was raised from the dead and resurrected by God to be made the glorious Son of God, victorious over death forever.

Jesus is all about victory, He is not about remaining down, He is looking for a result and a higher place for us to be, it is coming out of something that holds us down and entering into something new which lifts us above.
When you enter in by putting to death the deeds of the flesh, there is also an exit point which is Resurrection Life.

We still need to see that without the cross there would not be a Resurrection.
What does it mean to us? We need to go in by the way of the cross to see victory over the deeds of the flesh.

Without the entry into identifying with the death of Jesus on the cross, there would not be new life.

Resurrection power without the cross is counterfeit and is fake and Gods ways are not fake but true, so we need to go in to the entry and then exit by faith to the place of victory.

No one wants to be a fake and if there is offered a shortcut that bypasses God's way to victory, don't buy into it, it is a lie from the enemy offering the so called easy way to power, there is no automatic instant hit, no doorways without going by the cross, we preach Christ crucified. If your flesh is allowed to run rampant and rule it will gain ascendancy and dominate the power and the gift and the motivation will not be pure.

When our giftings operate from a mixture of motives, it can look good on the surface as it resembles the true in some ways; just like the counterfeit it can resemble the original. You don't want that, who wants to be a fake? Fakes all get found out eventually, an expert will at some point find the flaws and the fake characteristics; it will not pass the test of authenticity.

The sting of death is sin. So it is all about removing the sting, God doesn't want to leave us with the sting still inflicted in our mortal bodies, stings come from nasty creatures like scorpions, a very nasty evil creature.

Lazarus became sick and sunk down all the way to death before he received resurrection life.

Sometimes we sink down pretty low and we struggle with afflictions, addictions, secret sins, bad habits that just carry on for so long that we begin to accept that it is just part of who we are.
Well there is a hope and there is an answer. We do not set aside the grace of God, it is available in abundance, so lets appropriate it by faith in what Jesus has already accomplished for us on the cross.

John 11:23-26 (continuing on from our bible reading text)
23 But Jesus answered them, saying, "The hour has come that the Son of Man should be glorified.
24 Most assuredly, I say to you, unless a grain of wheat falls into the ground and dies, it remains alone; but if it dies, it produces much grain.
25 He who loves his life will lose it, and he who hates his life in this world will keep it for eternal life.
26 If anyone serves Me, let him follow Me; and where I am, there My servant will be also. If anyone serves Me, him My Father will honor.

There is always a trade off, an exchange in a purchase, God gave his Son to set us free and that was a trade of love on our behalf.

We need to enter into this place of exchange and receive the new, when the old is put away on the cross, just like Abraham it can look pretty bad, but Gods promise is sure and we can forget the failures of the past to take hold of the new future that has been purchased for us.

Yes there is a losing of a life, what a life! Our old life, which is also our God given right by choice to keep, we don't have to lay it down, we can keep our old ways, but really where does it get us? Into the Tomb?

Now we are not expected to be the Messiah like Jesus and take the whole weight of the sins of the world and suffer that way, we cannot, because we are not perfect and cannot satisfy the law, so our sacrifice would be rejected.

If Jesus did not go before us there would just be no way out of the tomb.

No it is a place of exchange, where we hand over our right to keep this life of sin and give it up to Jesus on the cross, He has already taken it, so it is finished and already dealt with, but we still need to make that choice and enter in and exit with His Resurrection Life to victory over the power of death - our sin.

Romans 6:1-14

1 What shall we say then? Shall we continue in sin that grace may abound?

2 Certainly not! How shall we who died to sin live any longer in it?

3 Or do you not know that as many of us as were baptized into Christ Jesus were baptized into His death?

4 Therefore we were buried with Him through baptism into death, that just as Christ was raised from the dead by the glory of the Father, even so we also should walk in newness of life.

5 For if we have been united together in the likeness of His death, certainly we also shall be in the likeness of His resurrection,

6 knowing this that our old man was crucified with Him, that the body of sin might be done away with, that we should no longer be slaves of sin.

7 For he who has died has been freed from sin.

8 Now if we died with Christ, we believe that we shall also live with Him,

9 knowing that Christ, having been raised from the dead, dies no more. Death no longer has dominion over Him.

10 For the death that He died, He died to sin once for all; but the life that He lives, He lives to God.

11 Likewise you also, reckon yourselves to be dead indeed to sin, but alive to God in Christ Jesus our Lord.

12 Therefore do not let sin reign in your mortal body, that you should obey it in its lusts.
13 And do not present your members as instruments of unrighteousness to sin, but present yourselves to God as being alive from the dead, and your members as instruments of righteousness to God.
14 For sin shall not have dominion over you, for you are not under law but under grace.

OK you see now that we have been given His resurrection life and the overcoming newness of life.
Sin does not have dominion over us any more. That is an established truth that we can appropriate by faith.
We need that reinforced into our thinking, like a brand new turban placed over our head that will shelter us from the reminder of our old habits.

Change sometimes seems so hard when you are ingrained in a pattern of behaviour, however change is good, especially when it means we have newness of life and not the same old habits and the same old place, but a new place of overcoming in life over our former ways.
Reckon yourself to be the new man, the new woman, who is not defeated and dragged down by filthy old clothes that have accumulated in your life from the wicked ways of this world that shrouds us in a dark cloud.

No! No longer! You can say it and agree with the Word of God and His promise that this is all going to change, this day onwards! Receive it, believe for it, make it your statement of faith, then start seeing yourself as God sees you - alive from the dead, made new, and changed by the power of God.
Mean business like Jesus, commanding the resurrection life to come forth and the death to be loosed.

It is time for your new day. No more of the old has-been of the past.
The future is Resurrection Life.

Some of us are like Joshua the High Priest, are the man or woman of God that are chosen for such a time as this.

Like Joshua you might be plucked from the fires and trials of this life and you may still be wearing those filthy clothes, God is in the process of plucking you out, calling you forth and it was no surprise to Him that you got burnt and filthy and that you ended up in the ash heap of life.

Others have come to the end of themselves, you've tried and tried, given it all your best shot only to have the dream and the future snatched away from you, this is very discouraging and it is hard to pick yourself up from this place and find a new lease of life.

Maybe some have created an Ishmael, this is what you have produced, you know you have conceived it, you operated by your own resources and you reasoned that by the appearance of the situation, this was the best way to go, as there did not seem to be any other way to produce a result.

You took the course, but in the end you know it was birthed an Ishmael, a product of the flesh, it resembled the father, it had the name on it, the genes were there that gave it an appearance of being right, but it was not the promised child, it was not conceived from above by faith in the miracle working power and that is the same power that raised Jesus from the dead.

Psalm 113:7-9
7 He raises the poor out of the dust,
And lifts the needy out of the ash heap,
8 That He may seat him with princes—
With the princes of His people.
9 He grants the barren woman a home,
Like a joyful mother of children.

Here is how God sees the situation and He is here now to offer you real Resurrection Life and take you higher, far above the place of death and the dusting that branded you. It is time to go the way of exchange and take hold of His Newness of Life, it is your rightful place in life, and it is your future.

We need to be lifted out of our ash heap in life; it is not something we can shake off easily, that is why Jesus came to save us, as we needed to be lifted out by a miracle.
Yes there is more to knowing a foundational truth and there is an application that comes from understanding and growing into what we learn by experience.
This Chapter lays a foundational truth and this gives us knowledge and we will not perish when we gain knowledge to our faith.
We now know we can appropriate this new life and in the next chapters we will see that there is walking into His ways, which doesn't happen without understanding His ways and how to walk this way.
We must also understand what the opposing forces are and how they operate to take us out.

He moves us forward with His wisdom that is very practical and can be applied to our situation – it is a now word for us - applicable for our unique time and place.

God's ways are higher than our ways.

Isaiah 55:8, 9
8 "For My thoughts are not your thoughts, Nor are your ways My ways," says the Lord.
9 "For as the heavens are higher than the earth,
So are My ways higher than your ways, And My thoughts than your thoughts.

CHAPTER 2

Our Dominion His Dominion

In the previous chapter we established that we have access to resurrection life, by the same Spirit that raised Jesus from the dead which was provided through the cross, this sacrifice gave us the right to enter in as we continue to believe and leave our former ways behind us.

This is now an established point of access for us to continue in our faith and find His Life and His Grace to become all that He has for us this side of eternity. Now is the time of salvation, to take hold of our rights as children of the Most High God.

Then we finished up in *Romans 6* dealing with the power of sin in our lives, it is now defeated and no longer has a hold on us, since Jesus put it to death on the cross.

The words describing this action are *"sin no longer has dominion over us"*.

Let's look at the effect of dominion, it is a ruling body, a governing entity, a force that has a legal right to rule and be above its subjects, or in the case of sin - victims of death.

When we come into the Kingdom of Jesus as our Head and Saviour, we are removed from that position of being under those ruling principles that dominated us and our behaviour, we are placed above their hold and that is the place intended, where we reign in this life.

We will examine the dominion of sin from another perspective and see how this dominion is set up and the workings within and how it operates.

Psalm 94:20, 21
20 Shall the throne of iniquity, which devises evil by law,
Have fellowship with You?
21 They gather together against the life of the righteous,
And condemn innocent blood.

By the law, how dare they use the law of perfection against those that are enslaved by their devices, the law will always condemn us when we fall short of perfection, so they have if you like, incriminating evidence that is against us and that means they now have dominion over us, because of the legal right to accuse and they have access through our weaknesses of the sinful nature.

Yes they gather together against the righteous, condemn innocent blood, the plan of this dominion is to take us out of the place of ruling above with Jesus to the place where they can have dominion over us again.

They are less concerned with people who are already under their rule, as they are not part of the Kingdom of God, the focus of their attack is on those who become, or are becoming part of the Kingdom that is above their rule, and they conspire to take them back down again.

These dominions attempt to use our very weaknesses to rule over us and keep us under the dominion of sin and this is a pathway of death, we know that we would remain in the tomb until Jesus came, who is the Resurrection and the Life and He cried out to us *"come forth"*.

It is the blood of Jesus that declares us innocent and we have the righteousness of God to cover us from condemnation.

So what do the deceivers do? Try to get us back into the old thought patterns of the life we lived, under the hold of sin, they remind us of who we are without Christ, get our focus off Jesus and back on ourselves, so we fall back into old habits, especially if we are striving to be righteous, struggling to be free, we will slip from our place when pressure is applied to a weak footing, we are no longer standing on the truth, but a lie which says we are not worthy and we are sinful, which we are when we have shifted away from our position of faith and standing that we hold in Christ.

Also, another plot for the schemers of wickedness to get us out of our rightful place, is to try to gain access into our thinking and behaviour through our weaknesses, they will try to locate undealt with areas of iniquity, which are strongholds they have over us, where they set up camp inside, they push the buttons and see if it will pull us into an area of sin.

So strongholds are connected to ruling thrones of iniquity where the enemy has access by legal right of the law, over an area in our life. You see that is what Satan uses to oppose us and why there are garments that are filthy. Now God is above all, He knows our very weaknesses and the areas of our lives that need development and He always has a plan that is above the schemes of the enemy and will make a way for us to overcome.

Psalm 94:16-23
16 Who will rise up for me against the evildoers?
Who will stand up for me against the workers of iniquity?
17 Unless the Lord had been my help,
My soul would soon have settled in silence.
18 If I say, "My foot slips,"
Your mercy, O Lord, will hold me up.
19 In the multitude of my anxieties within me,
Your comforts delight my soul.
20 Shall the throne of iniquity, which devises evil by law,
Have fellowship with You?

*21 They gather together against the life of
the righteous,
And condemn innocent blood.
22 But the Lord has been my defense,
And my God the rock of my refuge.
23 He has brought on them their own
iniquity,
And shall cut them off in their own
wickedness;
The Lord our God shall cut them off.*

Unless the Lord had been my help there would not be victory, if I say my foot slips, which I do, I slip, the Lords mercy will hold me up and offer me a way out when I cry out to Him in my time of slipping in weakness.
His righteousness is my defense and Jesus is my rock of refuge where I receive newness of life to overcome.

We may have a multitude of anxieties within our soul, because of what we have come through in the past and the trial of what tribulations we faced in this life, God has sent His comforter the Holy Spirit who is our helper to teach us to take hold of who we are in Christ and provide refreshing, to help us back on our feet again.

Who is going to stand up for you when you slip and fall into a pit?
Jesus will stand up and say *"come forth I am the resurrection and the Life whoever believes in Me will never die".*

So as in *Galatians 2:20* we live by what?
"the faith of the Son of God who loved us and died for us."
The Rock and our refuge.

Abraham our example of faith trusted God and when things looked very dead and hopeless, he trusted in God to bring forth what? A new life - a son Isaac, a promised child. The situation is impossible without God, but with God all things are possible. He gives life to a dead situation. It was completely by faith that Abraham and Sarah had the promised child, they were as good as dead like Lazarus, their ability to conceive, bring forth was in the tomb, wrapped up in grave clothes of the natural.

There was the deadness of Sarah's womb, no ability to conceive within, that is how we are before God brings His Newness of Life into our beings and it is Resurrection Life that is above dominion which attempts to keep us down. Don't settle for second best in this life when only the best will do, the work of the impossible, raising us up out of a dead situation comes by faith in the Son of God. Death spread to all mankind and has contained us all in that tomb, like Lazarus we are really dead.

When Lazarus met the Resurrection and the Life he no longer had to stay where he was - under it.

C'mon reckon yourself as being dead to sin but alive to God in Christ Jesus, which is a position of faith, take hold of the higher life that is available to us to rule and reign in this life. We don't have to let death reign anymore. Why? Because there is an abundance of grace available to us and we have the gift of Righteousness that gives us our position which is above. Note the correlation between
Romans 5:20 - when sin abounds grace abounds more - with -
Romans 5:16 - the gift comes from many offenses.

You see what Jesus did on the cross was He dealt with all of the offenses, so if you are thinking that in your case sin has run amuck, it has taken over, way out of control, in the too hard basket case.

No, you are not the impossible case, there is an abundance of grace available to sort out all of the mess we can create through our sins, the ruling dominions in the throne of iniquity may have devised the best cunning, devious plan to take you out and you fell for it hook line and sinker, it was the ultimate, the perfect storm to wreck your ship to bits, but God says He has provided an abundance of grace to sort it, already done on the cross, so we need to reckon that God will do what He promised, He will be able to make it good, absolutely all the way up again, you will be wearing that crown and say yes it is mine by the grace of God.

What about an exceeding greatness available to us, that should do the trick don't you think?

Ephesians 1:19-21
19 and what is the exceeding greatness of His power toward us who believe, according to the working of His mighty power
20 which He worked in Christ when He raised Him from the dead and seated Him at His right hand in the heavenly places,
21 far above all principality and power and might and dominion, and every name that is named, not only in this age but also in that which is to come.

Is that enough? That sounds like abundance.
His power is toward us who believe, that is what is available.
HUGE – exceedingly great.
Now get this He seated Him where? -
At His right hand in the heavenly places – far above?
Now you get it - dominions.

Ephesians 1:22, 23
22 And He put all things under His feet, and gave Him to be head over all things to the church,
23 which is His body, the fullness of Him who fills all in all.

Right! He is the Head and He is above all dominion, He sure was not going to stay down on that cross and then in that tomb.
His fullness fills us - His body all in all.

So we really have got Resurrection Life to the full - a bit like–*"same Spirit that raised Jesus from the dead gives life to our mortal body"* in *Rom 8:11.*
On earth we are His mortal body, with all of our limitations that we have been born with and now we are given the position of total victory, it is all there and our part now is to take hold of it by faith.

Ephesians 2:5, 6
5 even when we were dead in trespasses, made us alive together with Christ
(by grace you have been saved),
6 and raised us up together, and made us sit together in the heavenly places in Christ Jesus

So this is our rightful position in Christ, seated with Him - we are raised up together with Him and we rule and reign.

Yes it is together, we are not off somewhere on our own, ruling the universe with the flick of fingers and waving our hand thinking positive thoughts to change the world and its elements by some suggestion of our mind.

He is the Head of the Body and we are connected to Him and rule from that place where He is the King of kings and the Lord of lords.

Now you see it is by grace that we are saved, this is the great foundational truth of the reformation of the dark ages and it is an important foundational truth that we establish our faith on, notice that this was all completed when?
When we were dead in our trespasses, so on the cross this is a done deed completed already by Jesus, settled forever, this is the truth and our pass into glory, by the grace that is offered; which is all of the benefits that we can receive due to Jesus dying on our behalf.

You see this is our position and rightful place as it is already been accomplished for us, but do you think someone who is dead and still in the tomb is going to be functioning in ruling and reigning in life with Jesus?

He has made the way ready and we do have access to all that is freely given by faith in what Jesus did on the cross. When we are first saved we are brought forth out of the tomb and the grave clothes come off and we begin to walk forward in the newness of life.

Lets look at *Romans 8* again as we want to be living in *Romans 8* victory not caught up in the cycles of defeat of *Romans 7*, where you do not do the things that you want to do, you want to move into victory where you are a mature son – led by His Spirit.

Romans 8:17
17 and if children, then heirs—heirs of God and joint heirs with Christ, if indeed we suffer with Him, that we may also be glorified together.

You see that our position is granted to us, what comes next in this verse is *"if indeed we suffer with Him that we may also be glorified together"*.

The grain of wheat from *John 11:23-26*.
Jesus was the grain of wheat, the original one and He was the grain of wheat that came from above, perfect in every way, but He still had to die.

All other grains of wheat must come from the original strain of the grain of wheat who is Jesus. We are not the grain, but a grain from the grain.
We bear a likeness from Him. We can try to be the grain, but it won't produce perfect life, it will produce a flawed seed.

Like GM seeds that are modified, altered, they have the ability to produce taken from them, we have been genetically altered and need to go through Him and from Him to produce new life. Our very DNA is resurrected by the life of Jesus, we are now children of our Father God through Jesus.

We don't want to produce contaminated fruit or seeds that do not last and are dead, so we need to be transformed from decaying and corrupted seeds by the one who is perfect in every way - He is Jesus the King of kings and Lord of lords and may I say - *Seed of seeds*.

So if we are ruling and reigning, it is from the place of together with Him, seated in the Heavenly Realms and not dominated by the dominions of darkness.
The love of the Father is working through us when we rule and reign with Jesus, joint heirs with Christ, we are really connected to Him.

The next Chapter leads us more into to a real heart connection to God.

CHAPTER 3

New and Living Way

Heb 2:14-16
14 Inasmuch then as the children have partaken of flesh and blood, He Himself likewise shared in the same, that through death He might destroy him who had the power of death, that is, the devil,
15 and release those who through fear of death were all their lifetime subject to bondage.
16 For indeed He does not give aid to angels, but He does give aid to the seed of Abraham.

Jesus came in the flesh as a man and destroyed the powers that had the power of death and gave us release from the grip and fear that enslaved us.
So we enter into the Kingdom that is above the power of death and this is a place of victory, Jesus came to our aid with His Authority and the resurrection power to set us free.

We have a word of testimony that says this is so and we can declare to the opposition who we are and what we have received.

John 17:6
6 I have manifested Your name to the men whom You have given Me out of the world. They were Yours, You gave them to Me, and they have kept Your word.

We keep His word in our hearts, we hold onto His word, we enforce His word as true for our life.

John 17:14
14 I have given them Your word; and the world has hated them because they are not of the world, just as I am not of the world.

We have been given His word and the one that had the power of death over us hates the word, as it is our victory.

Romans 8:17
17 So then faith comes by hearing, and hearing by the word of God.

We receive His word, faith comes, we keep his word and we keep in faith.

Matthew 4:4
But He answered and said, "It is written, 'Man shall not live by bread alone, but by every word that proceeds from the mouth of God.' "

So we live by His Word, this is the word of faith, the word is living, the word is Jesus and we partake of Him.

It is a Rhema Word, a spoken word from God, it is alive, because it is a now word for our today, to shape our tomorrow by faith according to the word given to us.

John 17:20
"I do not pray for these alone, but also for those who will believe in Me through their word;

The word can also come through His chosen prophets and messengers, we are given His word, that we might live and that others may believe.

John 1:1
1 In the beginning was the Word, and the Word was with God, and the Word was God.

Jesus is the Word He is living and His life is in us when we receive His word.
He is Immanuel, God with us when we receive His word into our hearts.
Now let's look at our makeup, the compartments of our beings and how God is in us and His Word becomes part of who we are.

Hebrews 8:10
10 For this is the covenant that I will make with the house of Israel after those days, says the Lord: I will put My laws in their mind and write them on their hearts; and I will be their God, and they shall be My people.

So there is a *"put laws in mind"* and *"write laws in heart"* we have a mind of our souls and a heart centre of our beings and we are spirit beings.

Hebrews 9:1-11

Then indeed, even the first covenant had ordinances of divine service and the earthly sanctuary.
2 For a tabernacle was prepared: the first part, in which was the lampstand, the table, and the showbread, which is called the sanctuary;
3 and behind the second veil, the part of the tabernacle which is called the Holiest of All,
4 which had the golden censer and the ark of the covenant overlaid on all sides with gold, in which were the golden pot that had the manna, Aaron's rod that budded, and the tablets of the covenant;
5 and above it were the cherubim of glory overshadowing the mercy seat. Of these things we cannot now speak in detail.
6 Now when these things had been thus prepared, the priests always went into the first part of the tabernacle, performing the services.
7 But into the second part the high priest went alone once a year, not without blood, which he offered for himself and for the people's sins committed in ignorance;
8 the Holy Spirit indicating this, that the way into the Holiest of All was not yet made manifest while the first tabernacle was still standing.
9 It was symbolic for the present time in which both gifts and sacrifices are offered which cannot make him who performed the service perfect in regard to the conscience—

*10 concerned only with foods and drinks, various washings, and fleshly ordinances imposed until the time of reformation.
11 But Christ came as High Priest of the good things to come, with the greater and more perfect tabernacle not made with hands, that is, not of this creation.*

So first there was an Earthly Sanctuary that comes from our history on earth - this was the first covenant which had the limitations of the earthly, earthbound and from a lower order that is a copy of the original.

There are two compartments within the body of the temple but having earthly properties, where the priests of the old order practiced fleshly ordinances which cannot make those perfect in regard to the conscience.

We need a new covenant that is able to put the laws into the mind and write the laws in the heart of the believer and God is truly our God. When Christ came He offered the good things to come in the tabernacle not made by human hands and not of this earthly creation.

We need to find out how to bring the good things into our earthly place, where we are spirit beings that have a soul and live in a body that is material from this earth.

BODY - the outer court of the Sanctuary - we place ourselves and enter into Gods Courts. We submit ourselves for blessing – an earthly container.

SOUL – change of the mind - laws put in their mind, this is the holy place where there is light from the lampstand bringing revelation truth – a table where we partake of the knowledge - showbread is like foundational truths from the word that we are taught to show us who we are in Christ.

SPIRIT - The Holiest of all has purity of gold - the Golden Censor *(Prayers of Saints)* - Ark of the Covenant *(Presence of God and His Glory)* - Golden Pot with Manna *(Word from Heaven)* – Aarons staff that budded *(counsel, wisdom, prosperity)* Tablets of the Covenant *(written laws on their hearts)*.

Cherubim of Glory overshadows the Mercy Seat where we are accepted by God through the sacrifice of the perfect Lamb of God.

Only a brief overview of the elements – not intended to be complete, there is so much more to discover I believe.

The Holy Spirit indicates the way is open to the Most Holy Place, where the experience gets really holy and intimate, when we get to the heart and this is the place where two hearts beat as one, a place of relationship with our God. Our spirit is made alive and we can enter into Glorious Communion with God in the place of heart connection and this is our divine connection.

My feeble description cannot achieve the wonders of knowing God and His Glory of this most holy place, which now has been made open for us.
We can enter in boldly, because of the blood of Jesus and our confession, however, there is protocol and there is a reverence that you and I need to adhere to and grow to understand in our experiences with God and His Majestic and awesome presence.

I know the Father isn't going to grab you by the collar and pull you into the most holy place; this is part of the process of coming to know Him and the choice that we may willingly submit to Him and come to Him as an accepted son or daughter knowing His love.

There is a place on the way where we are shown who we are in Christ and what is available to us as believers. We can partake of the bread at the table, the shewbread shows us revelation truths that help us understand the principles of God, so we can enter into the spirit realm with understanding; in this place we can praise Him and make declarations of who we are and what we are shown.
There comes with revelation truth a measure of His wonderful presence and it is good to seek His presence and receive not by our own reasoning, but in a place of teachability; by the Spirit of Truth we receive knowledge on the reality of who He is and who we are in Christ.

Even at this wonderful place of knowledge and glorious truth accompanied by His wonderful presence there is so much more and He wants us to come higher up above even this incredible truth.

There is a love and intimacy that is above knowledge and when we progress in our relationship with Him, we enter into the holiest place and experience the love of God in a close bond in a throne room experience and this is where true worship takes place, where we enter into a progressively higher life and are changed forever.

Relationship with God is eternal and never ending, it is an endless life.

I will not go into detail on the elements of the most holy place, I don't pretend to know it all and there is much excellent teaching on these, it still is a place of discovery for me and perhaps you as well. We are growing up into this place of transformation and newness.

My aim is to point us to the place where we are changed by the Presence of God and His Glory and the deposit in our hearts will flourish.
In this place of becoming mature sons and daughters of God we develop a faith that will not be shaken; we can reach new levels and be led by His Spirit in greater measures.

The way is open, the invite is here for now, we can enter in to the fullness and be in a place beyond description that fulfills all of our dreams, and this is where the exchange is great, exceedingly great.

Hebrews 9:9, 10
9 It was symbolic for the present time in which both gifts and sacrifices are offered which cannot make him who performed the service perfect in regard to the conscience— 10 concerned only with foods and drinks, various washings, and fleshly ordinances imposed until the time of reformation.

If we remain dependent on our reasoning and the knowledge gained *(like we have got it all figured out now)* true as it is, we are directed by our mere knowledge and principles and we will not progress into knowing Him who is above all knowledge, where His love directs us to the perfect tabernacle.

Like formulas that become do this and do that, we cannot by rituals performed make us perfect in regard to conscience. Christ came - not of this creation - not of anything we can reason out and formulate - Christ comes to inhabit our hearts from above. We become the New Creation from above when we enter into His presence in the perfect tabernacle.

Hebrews 9:14
14 how much more shall the blood of Christ, who through the eternal Spirit offered Himself without spot to God, cleanse your conscience from dead works to serve the living God?

We don't want to be known as dead works people, we need to enter into the place where our conscience is cleansed from dead works *(rituals and religious practices that are external)* to serve the Living God.
No more rituals in the flesh in the earthly sanctuary we are now led by the Spirit of God.

Heb 10:2
2 For then would they not have ceased to be offered? For the worshipers, once purified, would have had no more consciousness of sins.

When we have a consciousness of sins we tend to want to make things right and the tendency is to do works from the earthly sanctuary of performance and striving, to make it good with God.

That's where we carry on with fixing, patching, stitching things up; this is straining by lots of sweat and labour.
Just receive His grace, God doesn't need a helping hand when it comes to supplying the Spirit and miracles.

Heb 10:9
9 then He said, "Behold, I have come to do Your will, O God." He takes away the first that He may establish the second.

We just need to enter into the will of God, there is a place we can go to have this written inside and then we can go out in the confidence of knowing His will, His instruction, the way to go in life.

Hebrews 10:14
14 For by one offering He has perfected forever those who are being sanctified.

Yes He has perfected us, so we now have access to the Heavenly, the good things from above that will cleanse our conscience, this is forever established already and we hold our place in Him.
Notice that we are among those who are being sanctified, now that sounds like change going on inside.
What can we now do with the position offered to us and the acceptance of God the Father? What does the Father seek, what is it He delights in and who does He love to be with?

John 4: 23, 24
23 But the hour is coming, and now is, when the true worshipers will worship the Father in spirit and truth; for the Father is seeking such to worship Him.
24 God is Spirit, and those who worship Him must worship in spirit and truth."

OK there is a requirement here, there is protocol if I can put it that way, but it is much more personal than that.
Yes there is reverence, but there is also a sweet communion and personal relationship with God by His acceptance and love towards us. The way is now opened to us through Jesus.

We are able to worship in spirit and truth in this place of acceptance where the Glory of God is in the Most Holy Place.
There is corporate worship and there is individual worship, each have there place and have their role in the Kingdom of God.

Revelation Knowledge is wonderful, I love receiving teaching and learning new truths in His word, what follows is understanding and then the application, experiencing to knowing - walking it out - that seems right doesn't it? We get to walk with God in our experience and growing up in Him.

Heb 10:19-23
19 Therefore, brethren, having boldness to enter the Holiest by the blood of Jesus,
20 by a new and living way which He consecrated for us, through the veil, that is, His flesh,
21 and having a High Priest over the house of God,

22 let us draw near with a true heart in full assurance of faith, having our hearts sprinkled from an evil conscience and our bodies washed with pure water.
23 Let us hold fast the confession of our hope without wavering, for He who promised is faithful.

That's right we have a boldness like faith from the truth received, we may enter the Holiest by the Blood of Jesus, that is our cover and Right Standing before God.

It is by a **New and Living Way**.

Draw near with a true heart or as other versions put it a sincere heart.
Now you see faith kicking in with a full assurance of faith.
Hearts sprinkled from an evil conscience, there is a way in and we go in when we are saved and it is open to us by the blood of Jesus and His sacrifice; we need to remain in this faith and not go back to earthly rituals to please the Father.

Keep in the New and Living Way where there is Life.

Thank God our bodies are washed with pure water, there is a baptism and that again is a position of the flesh where it is placed on the cross where Jesus took the sins of mankind.

Hold fast the confession of Hope, no matter what you are going through and if the road is long and the change just doesn't seem to happen, He who promised is faithful.

Avoid the wrong attitude which is found in - *Matthew 15:8*
8 These people draw near to Me with their mouth, And honor Me with their lips, But their heart is far from Me.

You see there is a way of doing all the right things, but not having a sincere heart, or the heart is far from God and that is why we need to draw near to God and find the sincere heart of true worship, there is a right way to go in and we all need to find how it works individually for each of us. As God knows us all individually – He made us, He knows who we are.

Heb 10:36-38
36 For you have need of endurance, so that after you have done the will of God, you may receive the promise:
37 "For yet a little while, And He who is coming will come and will not tarry.
38 Now the just shall live by faith; But if anyone draws back, My soul has no pleasure in him."

There is an endurance when we run the race, our motivation is faith, and we need to remain in faith to complete the course.
Don't give up!!!

What follows this verse is *Hebrews 11*, it is known as the faith Chapter - read in your own time it is inspiring.

Heb 7:16-26
16 who has come, not according to the law of a fleshly commandment, but according to the power of an endless life.
17 For He testifies: "You are a priest forever According to the order of Melchizedek."
18 For on the one hand there is an annulling of the former commandment because of its weakness and unprofitableness,
19 for the law made nothing perfect; on the other hand, there is the bringing in of a better hope, through which we draw near to God.
20 And inasmuch as He was not made priest without an oath
21 (for they have become priests without an oath, but He with an oath by Him who said to Him:
"The Lord has sworn
And will not relent,
'You are a priest forever
According to the order of Melchizedek'"),
22 by so much more Jesus has become a surety of a better covenant.
23 Also there were many priests, because they were prevented by death from continuing.
24 But He, because He continues forever, has an unchangeable priesthood.

25 Therefore He is also able to save to the uttermost those who come to God through Him, since He always lives to make intercession for them.
26 For such a High Priest was fitting for us, who is holy, harmless, undefiled, separate from sinners, and has become higher than the heavens;

We cant draw near to God according to the law *(fleshly commandment)* no one in the flesh is made perfect by the law.
We come to God through Jesus according to the power of what? – WOW – incredible - endless life.
Melchizadek - Jesus is a priest forever in the order of Melchizadek - we are kings and priests in Christ.
We need to connect and be related to the Endless Life which will save us to the uttermost.

This is the power that works in us, an endless life and just as Jesus continues forever, so do we, we are no longer under the earthly priesthood that died out, but we have come into an **ENDLESS LIFE** for eternity.

This will supersede our earthly birth and beginnings from this world, to receiving the Life not from this creation but from an endless life, Melchizadek has no beginning or end and no genealogy from this world.

Heb 3:1
Therefore, holy brethren, partakers of the heavenly calling, consider the Apostle and High Priest of our confession, Christ Jesus,

I can see that in worship, in spirit and truth we may move into a faith statement.
We are partakers of the heavenly calling, where is the High priest in the sanctuary, where is the place of real union? I believe it would be in the most holy place in His presence and where the cherubim of glory radiates.

Hebrews 4:9
9 There remains therefore a rest for the people of God.
There are no dead works in that place of rest in God we cease from our works and enter into the dimension of the Spirit.

Hebrews 4:11
11 Let us therefore be diligent to enter that rest, lest anyone fall according to the same example of disobedience.
NOW that is our part - diligent to enter the rest of God, it is not automatic; it involves our participation, an entering into.
Heb 4:12
12 For the word of God is living and powerful, and sharper than any two-edged sword, piercing even to the division of soul and spirit, and of joints and marrow, and is a discerner of the thoughts and intents of the heart.

Alright Gods Word when it comes to us has the ability to discern the thoughts and the intents of the heart, you see the living Word like a sword goes in to divide what is earthly, soulish and from a heart that is not sincere.
The word compares the intents of the heart to what is written on our hearts and what is put into our minds by the Spirit of God and that is our rest to receive Gods Word by faith and not by the works of rituals and performance of our own making.
We live by the word of God, it is alive and active in our life, so receive the word that can bring about change of heart and correct our thinking to the ways of God.

Heb 4:14
14 Seeing then that we have a great High Priest who has passed through the heavens, Jesus the Son of God, let us hold fast our confession.

Hold tightly onto what is yours by making a bold statement of the truth that is above any earthly powers.
Now let us look again to the great High Priest Jesus, He is our priest who goes in on our behalf to help us to be closer to God, when we are faced with our humanity and the weaknesses that are divided by the word of God there is another Throne that has the complete opposite effect on us by the previously mentioned, sinister dominions, operating in the *Throne of Iniquity*.

Hebrews 4:15, 16
15 For we do not have a High Priest who cannot sympathize with our weaknesses, but was in all points tempted as we are, yet without sin.
16 Let us therefore come boldly to the throne of grace, that we may obtain mercy and find grace to help in time of need.

The *Throne of Grace* - like the abundance of grace, it has all been provided for us to receive.

God wants us to come boldly and not hesitate due to our weaknesses, Jesus has made the provision and we need to take hold of this grace to help us overcome and be what God has established for us, by the Spirit of God in the provision of Resurrection Life that is Endless.

Where do we go when we know that all our failings are laid bare and the only hope is mercy and grace – the Throne of Grace.

Looking again in the most Holy Place, there is the mercy seat and perhaps there is a relationship to the throne of grace, the Glory of God is in that place and we are accepted by the blood of Jesus, you know we are changed in His presence and there is no doubt about it.

2 Corinthians 3:18
18 But we all, with unveiled face, beholding as in a mirror the glory of the Lord, are being transformed into the same image from glory to glory, just as by the Spirit of the Lord.

Yes there is a place we can go where there is real change and there is a new and living way for us to enter into an endless life.

That is the beauty of this relationship, we can go before Him as we are and ask Him to search our heart, sometimes He will bring His search light onto our hearts, especially when we are in the place of submission and surrendered to His ways.

He leads us into the way that is an endless life.

There is no condemnation here. Just a place of exchange where we are transformed into His likeness, just surrender those dark places of iniquity to Him and do the exchange.

Remember it is the Throne of Grace where we find mercy and help in our time of need – there is the mercy seat, the blood of Jesus will purify us and cleanse us from all unrighteousness and move us into His glorious light.

Our very weaknesses become places of new and endless places of life, so when we are faced with our shame and our impurities, it is the mercy of the Father to reveal these and then shower us in His Glory, forever changing our hearts and minds, we are transformed and free from the condemnation of the past, in contrast, the enemies of our soul will use our weakness to accuse us by the law and keep us bound in a cycle of defeat, but Jesus came to give us life and it is an endless life in abundance.

The important thing is not how you were or what you are today, come as you are into His presence, when you come to God enter into the place of worship and what you will be is who you really are in Christ by His grace and this is what determines your outcome.

Psalm 16:11
11 You will show me the path of life;
In Your presence is fullness of joy;
At Your right hand are pleasures
forevermore.

CHAPTER 4

Being in the Light

Is it here or is it there? Where are we supposed to be?
Heaven or Earth?

Luke 17:21
21 nor will they say, 'See here!' or 'See there!' For indeed, the kingdom of God is within you."

The Kingdom of God is within; it is within your heart.
That is where Christ is and we are seated with Him in the heavenly places when we allow His rule in our heart.
This is where we encounter God in our hearts in our spirit man; we worship God in Spirit and in Truth.
God is seeking true worshipers, where He lives and fills the temple with His presence to the full, the temple is your body, and this is where the tabernacle of God and His presence is if we allow Him in.

The laws are written on our hearts and placed in our mind, we are partakers of the endless life, not according to an earthly law that does not take away the consciousness of sins, and it is an endless life that fills our beings with the very presence of God and His glory that changes everything.

So the answer is perhaps both places at once or whatever, don't get hung up on where it is, as long as He is in your heart the rest will follow, He will take you there, where to? Glorious places that the mind cannot conceive and way above our wildest dreams.

What is Being in the Light all about?

Philippians 1:6
6 being confident of this very thing, that He who has begun a good work in you will complete it until the day of Jesus Christ;

Alright there is a beginning and a way through to completion, so it is being in the light of the good work going on inside us.

1 John 1:5-7
5 This is the message which we have heard from Him and declare to you, that God is light and in Him is no darkness at all.
6 If we say that we have fellowship with Him, and walk in darkness, we lie and do not practice the truth.
7 But if we walk in the light as He is in the light, we have fellowship with one another, and the blood of Jesus Christ His Son cleanses us from all sin.

John 1:4, 5
4 In Him was life, and the life was the light of men.
5 And the light shines in the darkness, and the darkness did not comprehend it.

There is no darkness in God and so no shadows of a mixture of good and bad, no shifting from the true and turning to a different way.
It is like Faith, where there is No Doubt or Unbelief present.

Being is like walking, we are walking in that place where we have life which energises and moves us forward, but it us who is walking and there is a light to show us the way forward, so we can walk with confidence knowing our light with the motivation of the love life in our being.
We shall look at a great friend of God, Moses who accomplished much deliverance for the people of God and saw many mighty miracles.

Exodus 3:1-6
Now Moses was tending the flock of Jethro his father-in-law, the priest of Midian. And he led the flock to the back of the desert, and came to Horeb, the mountain of God.
2 And the Angel of the LORD appeared to him in a flame of fire from the midst of a bush. So he looked, and behold, the bush was burning with fire, but the bush was not consumed.
3 Then Moses said, "I will now turn aside and see this great sight, why the bush does not burn."
4 So when the LORD saw that he turned aside to look, God called to him from the midst of the bush and said, "Moses, Moses!"And he said, "Here I am."

5 Then He said, "Do not draw near this place. Take your sandals off your feet, for the place where you stand is holy ground." 6 Moreover He said, "I am the God of your father—the God of Abraham, the God of Isaac, and the God of Jacob." And Moses hid his face, for he was afraid to look upon God.

Notice when Moses turned aside to look he saw the fire from heaven on top of the earthly, like two worlds in the same place.
Moses turned away from all of the distractions of this world and the pull of duty to see the Heavenly – the things from above do not conform to the rules of this world they work on a higher dimension.

God called to Moses. He is calling out to us to see the wonders of Heaven that take us out of the restrictions of this life.
Listen when He calls and when He comes into your day to day existence, if you turn aside and look and open your heart to Him you will see the sights of Heaven from the endless life above.

We need to turn aside from the status quo of life to catch the fire of God.
Eyes of faith look beyond the natural – where carnal man made objects and systems of this world just exist day to day.
We have the blueprint from heaven and it is laid out for us, now we just need to respond.

Notice that when Moses looked towards the place where God had appeared in a supernatural burning bush, this experience was over and above the natural.
Moses came to Holy Ground like moving into the zone, he was transferred in the Heavenlies to a Holy place where God dwells, we can take our earthly shoes off and take in the fire of God and His presence and walk a different way that is way above what we have known.

Exodus 4:10-14
10 Then Moses said to the LORD, "O my Lord, I am not eloquent, neither before nor since You have spoken to Your servant; but I am slow of speech and slow of tongue.
11 So the LORD said to him, "Who has made man's mouth? Or who makes the mute, the deaf, the seeing, or the blind? Have not I, the LORD?
12 Now therefore, go, and I will be with your mouth and teach you what you shall say."
13 But he said, "O my Lord, please send by the hand of whomever else You may send."
14 So the anger of the LORD was kindled against Moses, and He said: "Is not Aaron the Levite your brother? I know that he can speak well. And look, he is also coming out to meet you. When he sees you, he will be glad in his heart.

Moses had a lot of excuses; he only saw his own limitations and not Gods ability working in his life.

This is not a good response to God when he declares who you are in Christ and gives you His word for your life.

Exodus 4:24-26
24 And it came to pass on the way, at the encampment, that the LORD met him and sought to kill him.
25 Then Zipporah took a sharp stone and cut off the foreskin of her son and cast it at Moses' feet, and said, "Surely you are a husband of blood to me!"
26 So He let him go. Then she said, "You are a husband of blood!"—because of the circumcision.

Now we see in Moses a failure to adhere to the practices of God, if there is an uncircumcised heart and mind – Gods ways are not practiced. We see that Moses son is what he produced in the natural and this was uncircumcised and worldly.

Jesus did not come to bring us back to the earthly, He destroyed those works of death in us and He expects us to take on the newness of life that He has provided by His death on the cross.

Even if it is unpopular by the world's standards, as they want us to remain in worldly practices, if we are married to the world then we won't put on the new life it will be foreign and a clash of cultures for us.

Let's take heart from Moses and his example, look how shaky he was in the beginning and where he arrived in God, Moses became a great friend of God, speaking to God like face to face, spent 40 days and 40 nights on the mountain of the Lord, his face shined with the glory of God – he was a Glory of God carrier and then he led the people of God to the promised land out of the bondage of Egypt.

So if you think you have blown it with God and messed up and made lots of excuses with little faith, it is time to go up the mountain to be renewed.

Rom 2:29
29 but he is a Jew who is one inwardly; and circumcision is that of the heart, in the Spirit, not in the letter; whose praise is not from men but from God

Circumcision of the heart is the praise from heaven not from men, be careful not to be fearful and please mankind above God.

Romans 2:15, 16
15 who show the work of the law written in their hearts, their conscience also bearing witness, and between themselves their thoughts accusing or else excusing them) 16 in the day when God will judge the secrets of men by Jesus Christ, according to my gospel.

This is the conscience we need to follow the law written on our heart by the Spirit of God.

Moses had to make a sacrifice to stop the Angel of the Lord killing him which Moses wife performed reluctantly.

If we try to enter in to Gods Sanctuary by our own works, being uncircumcised of heart, then we are facing a fearful judgment as we are not covered by grace any longer, we attempt to please God in the flesh that will be subject to the letter of the law that does not measure up to the pure heart of the perfection that comes by the cross of Jesus Christ.

Draw near to God with a sincere heart – what is our heart condition like?
Go to the throne of Grace in time of need, we all need to, that is how it is and what we are like, we can be honest before God.
Psalms 40:1-8
I waited patiently for the Lord;
And He inclined to me,
And heard my cry.
2 He also brought me up out of a horrible pit,
Out of the miry clay,
And set my feet upon a rock,
And established my steps.

3 He has put a new song in my mouth—
Praise to our God;
Many will see it and fear,
And will trust in the Lord.

*4 Blessed is that man who makes the Lord his trust,
And does not respect the proud, nor such as turn aside to lies.
5 Many, O Lord my God, are Your wonderful works
Which You have done;
And Your thoughts toward us
Cannot be recounted to You in order;
If I would declare and speak of them,
They are more than can be numbered.
6 Sacrifice and offering You did not desire;
My ears You have opened.
Burnt offering and sin offering You did not require.
7 Then I said, "Behold, I come;
In the scroll of the book it is written of me.
8 I delight to do Your will, O my God,
And Your law is within my heart."*

Ever felt like you jumped out of the frying pan and then into the fire?

Why is that we go from crisis to crisis? We just get out of one mess, feel that relief, vow not to get into that type of trouble again and what happens we repeat a pattern, a cycle of defeat even though we do not intend to go there again.
It is like some type of magnetism that pulls us a certain way, we are back in again and moving to another location does not seem to fix the problem either, the grass is greener they say, but you find the same scenario with different players.

There must be an underlying stronghold that creates habit patterns, like a sub-conscious trigger loaded that goes off inside, bang off we go again, it draws us down that track.

Generational Strongholds that have become part of our identity gives the enemy access and a legal right to take away our blessings and removes our Authority, when iniquity resides in a certain area.

That's why we need the sword, the word of God to divide and highlight what is going on in the soul and bring us to a place where we can have this region dealt with by the power that is above all – a light shining in a dark place.

It is back again to the Throne of Grace, you will find that this throne or authority rules above the lower throne of iniquity, the throne above is seated above those dominions and there is a seat, called a mercy seat.

Hallelujah I need mercy and I need grace to get me out, as a matter of fact when I am in a pit and if I jump out where do I go? The pull of gravity draws me down into the fire, a bit like Joshua being snatched out of a fire.
God brings you up out of the horrible pit, because His Throne is above all and that is the only way out by His grace, if we try to jump, the pull that is in us, the weights of sins will drag us back down into the fire from out of that pan.

When your feet are stuck in miry clay, you just cannot move, you are stuck literally; you know when you are in that situation the only way out is up, being lifted up and out of there.

Take hold of His hand, accept the offer of grace that will lift you above your strongholds, you see that word is *"strong hold"*, it is a grip and it is the pits and the miry clay.
He will place your feet on a rock that is Jesus our Saviour, who is security for us, He is our redeemer.

Your steps are established by God when you are walking in step with Him and the weights of your past are removed, it is easier to move forward in steady fashion. Now the pull and the magnetism will be to the ways of God, which are above our ways and the plans of the enemy.

In *Psalm 40:8* we see the effects again of a circumcised heart, we delight to do His will and His law is in our heart, that is transformation and I believe that is the key to being in the light, you are changed on the inside where the Kingdom of God is within and this is when the magnetism lifts you above, you are drawn towards the place of ruling and reigning above the circumstances and the hold of the enemy. It is more than a process going on, it is a shift, it is a moving in our hearts from here to there, or up from here.

Growth is more about character, knowledge, faith and the more we position ourselves for the shift,
the more we can grow and accelerate forwards into Him. Acceleration to maturity is possible, the only thing stopping us from entering into the fullness which is already done and provided is our human limitations, weaknesses which Jesus has already dealt with on the cross.

The more we enter into the place of exchange which is the Throne of Grace, the more we can move forward towards the knowledge of Him and the fullness of what is provided.

Have I got this figured out to the full, by no means I am a novice, this is all new territory, but I see that there is a coming acceleration for the Body of Christ to enter into the fullness of mature sons of God. Now there has been individuals dotted through history that stood above the rest, but the heart of God is to see this transferred to the body corporate and even if there is a remnant, they will shake the planet for the Kingdom of God in the coming seasons of the Glory of God filling the whole earth.

Are you with me in this? Can you see what is coming?
This is what many prophets and great men and women of God are seeing coming forth.
You could think I am simply not good enough!

No none of us are and that is the problem trying to be good enough.
In Christ I am just right and I have all things that I need provided.
3 John 2
2 Beloved, I pray that you may prosper in all things and be in health, just as your soul prospers.
That's Gods will for your life to prosper, as your soul prospers it comes, so what is going on in the soul?

Philippians 2:12-16
12 Therefore, my beloved, as you have always obeyed, not as in my presence only, but now much more in my absence, work out your own salvation with fear and trembling;
13 for it is God who works in you both to will and to do for His good pleasure.
14 Do all things without complaining and disputing,
15 that you may become blameless and harmless, children of God without fault in the midst of a crooked and perverse generation, among whom you shine as lights in the world,
16 holding fast the word of life, so that I may rejoice in the day of Christ that I have not run in vain or labored in vain.
Work out your salvation with fear and trembling, this is something to be sober with, we can't afford to be slack in our faith and let it slip away, but make an effort to enter into the faith that God is working in us and that is His good will and pleasure.

That is having a pure heart that has Gods laws written into it.

Shining like stars in a crooked and perverse generation, without God we are crooked and perverse, with Him we shine like the stars or lights of the night in the world of darkness.

Crooked is like something that has a twist in it, so it was straight at one point but then it got twisted, like we put our twist on something.

Galatians 3:1-7
O foolish Galatians! Who has bewitched you that you should not obey the truth, before whose eyes Jesus Christ was clearly portrayed among you as crucified?
2 This only I want to learn from you: Did you receive the Spirit by the works of the law, or by the hearing of faith?
3 Are you so foolish? Having begun in the Spirit, are you now being made perfect by the flesh?
4 Have you suffered so many things in vain—if indeed it was in vain?
5 Therefore He who supplies the Spirit to you and works miracles among you, does He do it by the works of the law, or by the hearing of faith?—
6 just as Abraham "believed God, and it was accounted to him for righteousness."
7 Therefore know that only those who are of faith are sons of Abraham.

OK so the Galatians were part of the early church that was seeing God move in signs and wonders and the maturity level of this church would be quite good compared to our times I would think.
So they had some things sorted, like the gifts and character, moving beyond the foundations and on to the deeper walk in God. So how would an enemy deal with that level of maturity in believers?

If you can't get them to fall into sin, put them back under the law by developing perfection by works of the flesh. Now their hearts are moving away from dependence on the work of the cross and faith to efforts of the flesh or human ability, independent of God. Legalism always will falter due to some human weakness, as we are not perfected outside the Spirit of God performing miracles of transformation in out hearts and minds, a weakness that can easily occur in this case could be the pride of self righteousness.

We need to position ourselves for miracles and the supply of the Spirit of God, which moves us to our rightful place in Christ by His grace and by our faith in what has already been done.

Ephesians 4:11-15
11 And He Himself gave some to be apostles, some prophets, some evangelists, and some pastors and teachers,

12 for the equipping of the saints for the work of ministry, for the edifying of the body of Christ,
13 till we all come to the unity of the faith and of the knowledge of the Son of God, to a perfect man, to the measure of the stature of the fullness of Christ;
14 that we should no longer be children, tossed to and fro and carried about with every wind of doctrine, by the trickery of men, in the cunning craftiness of deceitful plotting,
15 but, speaking the truth in love, may grow up in all things into Him who is the head—Christ—

We need each other and the ministry of those who are gifted to equip us to move to maturity from wrong doctrine and the trickery of men who would lead us astray, by their cunning deceptions.

Yes so there is a growing up to do and if we hear the word spoken in love this will motivate us to maturity and being subject to the Head – Christ.

There is a time coming and I really think that God wills that the Body of Christ would reach a level of maturity that instead of needing constant fixing and restoring,
a significant number would rise up and be effective ministers in the community and the great harvest field of mankind.

Ephesians 3:9, 10
9 and to make all see what is the fellowship of the mystery, which from the beginning of the ages has been hidden in God who created all things through Jesus Christ;
10 to the intent that now the manifold wisdom of God might be made known by the church to the principalities and powers in the heavenly places,

OK you see that as we grow up into Him, we live by the created new man in Christ and this was a mystery and to some degree still is, as is the miraculous; the manifold diversity of the giftings of the Body of Believers will shine in this world in the wisdom of God and the dominions and powers in the heavenly places from their throne of iniquity will be powerless to stop His Church, as His will is done on earth and His Kingdom comes.

It is being in the light and that is the place of breakthrough.

CHAPTER 5

Up from Here

Let's look at our friend and our example of faith in Abraham and see his transition from one place to another.

Genesis 12:1-4
Now the Lord had said to Abram:"
Get out of your country,
From your family
And from your father's house,
To a land that I will show you.
2 I will make you a great nation;
I will bless you
And make your name great;
And you shall be a blessing.
3 I will bless those who bless you,
And I will curse him who curses you;
And in you all the families of the earth shall be blessed."
4 So Abram departed as the Lord had spoken to him, and Lot went with him. And Abram was seventy five years old when he departed from Haran.

Abraham left his home/idols/heritage/influence of the old life/generational bonds to a land that God showed him, a land of promise, and a land for the future, free from the past.

Genesis 12:7, 8
7 Then the Lord appeared to Abram and said, "To your descendants I will give this land." And there he built an altar to the Lord, who had appeared to him.
8 And he moved from there to the mountain east of Bethel, and he pitched his tent with Bethel on the west and Ai on the east; there he built an altar to the Lord and called on the name of the Lord.

Abraham worshiped God between a place called Ai towards the east and the place of Bethel, *"Gods House"* to the west. God has led him out of his former life to go to another place where there are blessings, he had to leave the past behind and all of the pulls of the strongholds of his heritage, as they would not allow him to be positioned for blessing.

So it is with us, God called us out of our past where there are pulls to the place of defeat, where iniquity rules over us from within, when we have these influences removed we are free to receive and are re-positioned in another place of authority and this takes place within our hearts and minds where the Kingdom of God now operates, unrestricted moving us into the place of blessings.

It is interesting that Abraham positioned himself between two places, on the east we have *Ai*, described as a *"place of refuse"* and on the west we have *Bethel* described as the *"House of God"*.

As a noun, *'refuse'* is waste, or garbage that is discarded.
[http://www.vocabulary.com/dictionary/refuse]

That is what it is like sometimes in our life as there are two sides that want to pull us towards their rule and their influence.

We need to worship God even when there is a pull away from Him going on inside us back towards the place of refuse. When we enter the throne of grace and enter into worship and we are in that place where Gods' presence resides, that is where great transition occurs. Do you think when we are yielded to God and His presence fills us that the pull towards our past life of refuse will overcome?

Absolutely not, remember the abundance of grace that is way more than the offenses, when we are there in the heavenly realms seated with Jesus Christ, our new identity is superimposed on our old identity and we take on His likeness, to be an overcomer and this is newness of life, being in the light is where light overtakes the darkness of our soul and our hearts are filled with the Kingdom of God, there is a delight to do his will, His laws are now written on our hearts and that is now the power of our magnetism that lifts us up and places our feet on a rock, we are not going to fall into the fire from this position.

Now that is where we are at, and that is where Abraham was at when he camped in between the two positions.

Abraham or Abram as he was known then, obeyed God and walked away from his past. However, the past can still reside in our minds and in our hearts, you know we grew up with it and it was part of who we were and a place of familiarity.

You see when Abram pursued God and worshiped him, at a point of breakthrough, God changed his name and gave him a new name and that is his new identity and destiny which is no longer based on his past life, Gods destiny is the original plan for your life, before you entered the fallen world and were shaped by its influences and pulls into iniquity.

There is a place in our heart that wants to follow God, a longing to belong in the House of God, however it is unfamiliar and it takes time to get to know God and His ways. When we enter His presence and receive His love we embrace the new and forget the old.

John 14:23
23 Jesus answered and said to him, "If anyone loves Me, he will keep My word; and My Father will love him, and We will come to him and make Our home with him.

The house of God is like a home and when we position ourselves wherever we are in worship to God, we keep His word in our hearts that says who we really are in Christ, then the Fathers' love is drawn towards us and the Father and Jesus make their home inside our heart and when this happens we are no longer in the sway of our past, but positioned in the place of His Kingdom. There is a shift inside our beings to where Gods glory and presence will shine through our hearts and we have the newness of life and not the deadness of a dominion of sin.

Refuse the refuse of Ai, press on to your God given destiny, no need to look back, we don't want to be a pile of salt like Lots wife, if we yearn for the past maybe God will need to pour salt on us, it is a purifier.

Psalm 103:8-13
8 The Lord is merciful and gracious,
Slow to anger, and abounding in mercy.
9 He will not always strive with us,
Nor will He keep His anger forever.
10 He has not dealt with us according to our sins,
Nor punished us according to our iniquities.
11 For as the heavens are high above the earth,
So great is His mercy toward those who fear Him;
12 As far as the east is from the west,
So far has He removed our transgressions from us.

*13 As a father pities his children,
So the Lord pities those who fear Him.*

OK are you getting it? There is mercy available to us and it is great, notice that *"as far as the east is from the west"*, he removes our transgressions from us. Yes there is Ai in the east and the House of God in the west, you see what happens and how far His grace goes that will move us from one extreme place to another that is opposite and that is like how God is, light as opposed to darkness, when we enter into His Kingdom there is going to be a displacement of the darkness by the light. Circumcision of the heart is like the effect of no more consciousness of sins, they have been removed.

Deuteronomy 6:4, 5
4 "Hear, O Israel: The Lord our God, the Lord is one!
5 You shall love the Lord your God with all your heart, with all your soul, and with all your strength.
And this is the greatest commandment, of all of the commandments if you get this one going, the rest are going to follow.

Deuteronomy 6:6-9
6 "And these words which I command you today shall be in your heart.
7 You shall teach them diligently to your children, and shall talk of them when you sit in your house, when you walk by the way, when you lie down, and when you rise up.

8 You shall bind them as a sign on your hand, and they shall be as frontlets between your eyes.
9 You shall write them on the doorposts of your house and on your gates.

There it is, these words shall be in your heart, remember the word of God and by the word of God we live, the word of God is given to us and the Kingdom of God is within.

Now you see a putting into the mind and a writing in the heart, the circumcision of God is in the heart, in the Spirit – it is not of the letter that kills, having a knowledge about God and knowing some scriptures is not the same as having a heart for God. There is a way to enter in and it is a new and living way and we can exit the old rituals of the flesh that cannot make us perfect, they only can bring incriminating evidence against us by the throne of iniquity that has a hold over us.

However, when Jesus cried out with great compassion *"come forth"* you came out of the place of bondage and next the grave clothes come off and the cloth about your head comes off where your mind is.

There is a discipline and a process of renewal where the new replaces the old and overtakes the whole man – body, soul and spirit.

1 Thessalonians 5:23, 24
23 Now may the God of peace Himself sanctify you completely; and may your whole spirit, soul, and body be preserved blameless at the coming of our Lord Jesus Christ.
24 He who calls you is faithful, who also will do it.

That is the plan of God to sanctify you completely, why? It is for your benefit that you no longer be held down and under.

Hebrews 12:5-9
5 And you have forgotten the exhortation which speaks to you as to sons:
"My son, do not despise the chastening of the Lord,
Nor be discouraged when you are rebuked by Him;
6 For whom the Lord loves He chastens, And scourges every son whom He receives."
7 If you endure chastening, God deals with you as with sons; for what son is there whom a father does not chasten?
8 But if you are without chastening, of which all have become partakers, then you are illegitimate and not sons.
9 Furthermore, we have had human fathers who corrected us, and we paid them respect. Shall we not much more readily be in subjection to the Father of spirits and live?

The Fathers Discipline is good, you see you are *"fearfully and wonderfully made"* read in *Psalm 139*, God knows you better than anyone including you and knows what is best for you.

He knows how you tick and He can tune all of the parts so you chime and there is a harmonious sound.

The sword of his word does cut at times, like circumcision there has to be a cutting away to remove the dead wood, the bad growth, you know how this works and it is for our best. Let's be in subjection to the Heavenly Father of our spirits and live.

1 John 2:15-17
15 Do not love the world or the things in the world. If anyone loves the world, the love of the Father is not in him.
16 For all that is in the world—the lust of the flesh, the lust of the eyes, and the pride of life—is not of the Father but is of the world.
17 And the world is passing away, and the lust of it; but he who does the will of God abides forever.

If our love is directed towards the things of the world it quickly converts from Gods peaceful purity to a driven lust of life and like all addictions can never be satisfied, there is always another big hit out there somewhere and this will be the chasing of rainbows with no end and no pot of gold, only the continuous taunting of the allusive bait that dangles in front of our eyes.

IDOLS are crafted objects that capture our hearts and they occupy our attention becoming worship.
If anything comes between us and God that we place above the ways and commandments of God, then it has become an idol and holds a position of authority over areas of our life.

Idols of the heart allow access and the influence of governing forces of darkness to mould our future and withhold the blessings of God.
If we are not in subjection to the Spirit of God and His leading and our focus is shifted away from God, then the lure of this world will pull us under subjection to its rule.

The crafty fisherman knows there is a way to allure and draw the big fish in and shiny bait is a choice method to capture the fish and hook them in.

Similar in method is the lust of the eyes, through what is appealing to the senses and captures the imagination and attention of the viewer, like advertising, will make use of something that sells and draws in the lust of the flesh. Girls, Gold and Glitter or Glory they say and what instruments they are, but you see each instrument in its origin is neutral, so it is the intention and the purpose of the instigator behind the tools used that is source of evil.

The pride of life is a different beast as it is something that is less outward and sensual, it is an internal drive with the have at all costs attitude for fame and fortune. Again the instruments and powerful positions in itself are not wrong, but the corruption of the motivation of the heart is where the downfall and destruction lies.

Carnal thinking gets you into this mode of motivation and it is simply a heart that is separate from the love of the Father and operating for selfish gain and ambition, with vanity it wants to make a name for itself, there is no love there, only a manipulation of people for its own selfish purposes.

When we have the Love of the Father we will see others through Gods eyes and this love will never fail and is pure. We can see people and worldly things through the light of His love and this won't allow the instruments to be used for corruption.

Let the light of His love shine through for a whole new way of living.

1 John 3:1-3
Behold what manner of love the Father has bestowed on us, that we should be called children of God!
Therefore the world does not know us, because it did not know Him.

2 Beloved, now we are children of God; and it has not yet been revealed what we shall be, but we know that when He is revealed, we shall be like Him, for we shall see Him as He is.
3 And everyone who has this hope in Him purifies himself, just as He is pure.

When we are like the one whose motivation is love, then the light of His love will shine through, changing our desires towards good things and the appeal of the world will lose its grip on us.

1 John 5:18,19
18 We know that whoever is born of God does not sin; but he who has been born of God keeps himself, and the wicked one does not touch him.
19 We know that we are of God, and the whole world lies under the sway of the wicked one.

There is a life that is placed in us that enables us to resist the wickedness, this is real change and empowering from above, but notice it is within our very hearts, when we have the empowering birthed into us from God we can keep ourselves and the evil can no longer sway us and keep us under its alluring lusts for more.

Ephesians 3:14-21
14 For this reason I bow my knees to the Father of our Lord Jesus Christ,

15 from whom the whole family in heaven and earth is named,
16 that He would grant you, according to the riches of His glory, to be strengthened with might through His Spirit in the inner man,
17 that Christ may dwell in your hearts through faith; that you, being rooted and grounded in love,
18 may be able to comprehend with all the saints what is the width and length and depth and height—
19 to know the love of Christ which passes knowledge; that you may be filled with all the fullness of God.
20 Now to Him who is able to do exceedingly abundantly above all that we ask or think, according to the power that works in us,
21 to Him be glory in the church by Christ Jesus to all generations, forever and ever. Amen.

You see the transformation process at work; we are strengthened with might by His Spirit in our inner *BEING*.
We are family, of the family of Heaven; we have the Name of the Father, our God. Now notice again Christ may dwell in our hearts by faith, there it is, going on in our hearts and it is by faith.
What happens when we come to God and spend time in His presence is we will know the love of God that surpasses knowledge, here is a process and we experience the filling with the fullness of God.

What happens is we have moved to the place of blessing like Abraham, we worshiped God and our hearts are in the house of God, we might be situated between east and west, but where is our heart?

When by faith Christ dwells inside, we are seated with Him in the heavenly realms. What happens when the Word of God is in our hearts and minds – faith comes, God does exceedingly abundantly above all we can ask or think according to His power that is at work in us.

We can position ourselves to be in and then be translated to the place of blessing – there is a being in the light in God.

John 15:1-9
"I am the true vine, and My Father is the vinedresser.
2 Every branch in Me that does not bear fruit He takes away; and every branch that bears fruit He prunes, that it may bear more fruit.
3 You are already clean because of the word which I have spoken to you.
4 Abide in Me, and I in you. As the branch cannot bear fruit of itself, unless it abides in the vine, neither can you, unless you abide in Me.
5 "I am the vine, you are the branches. He who abides in Me, and I in him, bears much fruit; for without Me you can do nothing.

6 If anyone does not abide in Me, he is cast out as a branch and is withered; and they gather them and throw them into the fire, and they are burned.
7 If you abide in Me, and My words abide in you, you will ask what you desire, and it shall be done for you.
8 By this My Father is glorified, that you bear much fruit; so you will be My disciples.
9 "As the Father loved Me, I also have loved you; abide in My love.

You see the Father at work pruning like circumcision, He skillfully works with the precision of the Master, He knows our intricate beings and every detail of our life and future, He cuts away the dead stuff out of our lives and frees up the new life to grow up in its place.

We need to abide in Him (Jesus) He is our life source and the way to the love of the Father which shines out in this world. His love is written in our hearts and taught into our minds and we now can walk in the light of this love. This is revolutionary, it is mind blowing in the cleanest and healthiest and most transforming way imagined – what a life we have in God.

Keeping that word is holding on to the word of life, no matter what we are going through we have His word and this is truth.

We can set up camp like Abraham in the place between the House of God and place of our past and whatever is holding us back and enter into worship, thanking God for His word and promises, when God comes and it actually really is us moving to where He is, in the place that He has already opened up for us and made the way ready. We are connected to the Father and Jesus and we know the Spirit of God is already in us, it is like a shift into the House of God where His Glory is and guess what, all things are possible in that place.

Moses looked towards the fire of God and went to where he was able to hear or experience more of Gods' Glory and he received instruction and His destiny in that place. Abraham received a new name and the vision of His future and the promises of God and he prospered greatly in the blessings of God.

We are blessed with all spiritual blessings.

Ephesians 1:2-6
2 Grace to you and peace from God our Father and the Lord Jesus Christ.
3 Blessed be the God and Father of our Lord Jesus Christ, who has blessed us with every spiritual blessing in the heavenly places in Christ,
4 just as He chose us in Him before the foundation of the world, that we should be holy and without blame before Him in love,

5 having predestined us to adoption as sons by Jesus Christ to Himself, according to the good pleasure of His will,
6 to the praise of the glory of His grace, by which He made us accepted in the Beloved.

We are there because it is Gods good pleasure to have us there, He predestined us to be there, Time is not a factor in the Heavenly Realms, so there is that already done place of acceptance by Father God, we just need to receive what He has already provided for us and allow the adoption of His ways and His Name take place inside our hearts.

CHAPTER 6

Love of the Father

PSALM 103:1-3
1 Bless the LORD, O my soul;
And all that is within me, bless His holy name!
2 Bless the LORD, O my soul,
And forget not all His benefits:
3 Who forgives all your iniquities,
Who heals all your diseases,

There are an abundance of benefits when you are in the family of God and one liberating benefit in the blessings of God is having your iniquities forgiven.
The very next verse has a corresponding benefit that seems to be associated with forgiveness and that is having your diseases healed.

Is there a correlation between iniquity having a hold on us and being afflicted by disease? Possibly, in some cases where sin has taken root and set up a dominion within your soul, there is a corresponding affect on your health resulting in disease. When our soul goes down an unhealthy track, the negative affects on our emotions and memories may trigger a breakdown in the bodies' immune defense systems.

Can we therefore say iniquities dealt with then diseases dealt with?

The account of Jesus and the infirmed man at the pool of Bethesda, Jesus prayed for this mans healing and later had some advice for him and a warning.

John 5:14
14 Afterward Jesus found him in the temple, and said to him, "See, you have been made well. Sin no more, lest a worse thing come upon you."

It appears that there is definite link to getting your sins sorted out and receiving healing.

Psalm 103:4, 5
4 Who redeems your life from destruction, Who crowns you with loving kindness and tender mercies,
5 Who satisfies your mouth with good things,
So that your youth is renewed like the eagle's.

More benefits of belonging to Gods Kingdom is being redeemed from the pathway to destruction.

After going down a track of destruction there is a lot of damage and wasted years, but God will renew our youth like the eagles and this is like being on the right path as you will be above the influences that were able to take you down the path of destruction.

You want to fly to the heights with freedom without being pulled down by the weight of iniquity, it's a lot of extra baggage that you can do without and will wear you down into the scrap heap.

He fills our desires with good things – desires that are right.
Iniquities are like a diet of filling up constantly with bad things and God wants to turn that around so that your mouth is filled with the good things of life, that bring health to your body.

The Throne of Iniquity has the legal right to rule over those that are under its sway and influence.
Iniquity has an access to the point of entry to sway your thinking, pull you down and drive you to destruction.

Driven behaviour is overwhelming and has a lot of momentum and push power to drive you in a wrong direction like an out of control freight train, you have seen those movies, very difficult to contain.
Addictions and lust are driving forces that push you into paths of destruction.

Psalm 107:17
17 Fools, because of their transgression,
And because of their iniquities, were afflicted.

If iniquity rules then this leads to disease as the behaviour is unhealthy and ultimately will bring a breakdown in quality of life.
Lifestyle – adverse to your health, unhealthy choices – like nutrition to our body – there is nutrition of the soul.
In *Psalm 103* at the opening we see King David in his element and place of strength to bring revival, as he praises the Lord and how much does he give towards God?

Bless the Lord – oh my soul and all that is within me.

He is telling his soul, directing his soul to bless the Lord and it is from the whole man.

Iniquity will shut you down, kills the vibrancy of the personality from the weight of its rule and domination. The result brings a crippled inside, due to oppression and out of control emotions. Joy and healthy expression has been stolen.

The soul has the ability to set up a wall of protection after suffering from traumatic experiences to numb the pain and block the memory from bringing up grief continually, the soul will want to cover the sin and the serious consequences of its fallen behaviour and then there is the guilt of failure and missing the mark that your sub-conscious will also suppress.

So these negative emotions and blocking of memories is kind of like denial and it creates an unhealthy balance like disharmony in our beings, which in due course affects our physical body.

We were created to be carriers of Gods light and this light of life is healthy for our beings, so when darkness resonates inside it results in system breakdown.
We need to counter the negative effects of iniquity by being filled with the light of Gods presence, so worship opens us up to a positive input and light will always dispel darkness.

Love the Lord with all of your strength, receive His grace and allow a shift of your focus to give all.

Turn your eyes on the One who is the changer of hearts.

All that is within me – my heart – what is your focus – what owns you?
Worship your way out of your circumstances and weakness.

Forget not all of his benefits – promises – confession – declare the word of God for your life and reckon yourselves changed to who God says you are.

Psalm 107:41
41 Yet He sets the poor on high, far from affliction,
And makes their families like a flock.

OK we were poor without His benefits, but now in Christ we may be placed where? Again it is in the high places, a position above the forces that bring affliction. Once we were under it, but now we have access to grace that will bring us above the place of suffering and subjection.

Psalm 94:20
Shall the throne of iniquity which devises evil by LAW
Have fellowship with you?

How do these devious creatures from the hideous throne of iniquity have access into our lives?
Well through the tool of iniquity, a sinful lifestyle and mindset that brings us down to their level.
Why?

Because the law brings judgment and removes us from the benefits of God.
So here is the question do they have fellowship with you? What is it like?
By being like minded and having the same kind of heart in darkness that is separate to God's love, having a focus on the lust for things and power.

Isaiah 41:23, 24
23 Show the things that are to come hereafter,
That we may know that you are gods;
Yes, do good or do evil,
That we may be dismayed and see it together.
24 Indeed you are nothing,
And your work is nothing;
He who chooses you is an abomination.

Well what happens with our freedom of choice is that we are the god of our own destiny, it is our choice, our right to go the way of our darkest imagination or do some good deeds when it suits, blow the trumpet of doing good deeds to people, or you might have a nice set of rules to live by. What happens your works are nothing without God, whatever you achieve are dead works, carnal and an abomination. That's harsh you say! It would appear to be harsh on the surface, superficially, works of the flesh appear to be good deeds, but without God, there is no eternal value and the true measurement of agape love will always find humanistic values coming up lacking and corrupted in some way, which is darkness without the true light shining through the heart intent.

A law unto ourselves – shifts to suit itself into situational ethics – if you are self righteous, then you come under the measurement of the law and you will always fall short when you are independent of God and His ways.

Only by grace you are saved and by grace you are enabled to live righteously.

We were born to have fellowship with God, this is a healthy lifestyle and will fill our beings with Gods goodness which is true and everlasting.

1 John 1:1-4
That which was from the beginning, which we have heard, which we have seen with our eyes, which we have looked upon, and our hands have handled, concerning the Word of life—
2 the life was manifested, and we have seen, and bear witness, and declare to you that eternal life which was with the Father and was manifested to us—
3 that which we have seen and heard we declare to you, that you also may have fellowship with us;
and truly our fellowship is with the Father and with His Son Jesus Christ.
4 And these things we write to you that your joy may be full.

Life and Joy is what life is meant to be about, not struggle and striving and sweating to make it right in our own eyes.

1 John 6, 7
6 If we say that we have fellowship with Him, and walk in darkness, we lie and do not practice the truth.
7 But if we walk in the light as He is in the light, we have fellowship with one another, and the blood of Jesus Christ His Son cleanses us from all sin.

How do the evil powers of darkness have fellowship with us?
By a connection from within and evil desires are being walked out through our actions.
How do we walk in the Light?
When we walk with Him by fellowshipping, worship, praying in the spirit and giving our all to Him as Lord of our lives, by following the leading of His Spirit and the direction of His Word and allowing our desires to be inspired by Gods love.

What is our covering and what positions us above workers of iniquity?
The blood of Jesus this is what cleanses us, there is power in the blood that defies our knowledge and is able to declare us righteous above the accusations of the cruel evil dominion that would otherwise find us guilty by the law, they are fault finders and haters of mankind and they only want to see us punished and tortured because of our sins.
They are completely black hearted with no compassion or mercy.

They just want to condemn and bring accusations when we do sin, to try to bring us back under by the law and out of the grace offered by God.
Jesus has innocent blood and we are covered by His blood.
Praise God for His kindness and compassion towards us.

Isaiah 33:20-24
20 Look upon Zion, the city of our appointed feasts;
Your eyes will see Jerusalem, a quiet home,
A tabernacle that will not be taken down;
Not one of its stakes will ever be removed,
Nor will any of its cords be broken.
21 But there the majestic LORD will be for us
A place of broad rivers and streams,
In which no galley with oars will sail,
Nor majestic ships pass by
22 (For the LORD is our Judge,
The LORD is our Lawgiver,
The LORD is our King;
He will save us);
23 Your tackle is loosed,
They could not strengthen their mast,
They could not spread the sail.
Then the prey of great plunder is divided;
The lame take the prey.
24 And the inhabitant will not say, "I am sick";
The people who dwell in it will be forgiven their iniquity.

When we have the Lord resident in our heart, really we are dwelling in His city of promise and protection. His tabernacle is a place in our heart where we have allowed Gods rule and Kingdom to set up and pour out blessings that we won't be able to contain.
These verses are all about the promised land blessings, with broad rivers and streams of Gods Spirit flowing and creating restoration and prosperity wherever the Spirit moves.

In this place where God rules, He is our judge and not an accuser that brings condemnation, but words of instruction giving life and direction.
His law written on our hearts and placed in our minds establishes our steps on a solid foundation for success. Jesus is the King of kings and when we are under His rule there is no oppression that can conquer us, but liberty and security with great peace.

The enemies sophisticated battle ships will no longer have access into our life. Notice the majestic Lord will save us, He is above all dominion and the opposing darkness will bow and grovel and squirm in His almighty presence.

The lame take the prey now – we can plunder the enemies camp when God is ruling in our hearts and His Kingdom is established in our lives, no battle resistance attack will penetrate the fortress of the Lord our God who is a strong tower and protection from ruling forces of evil that attempt to bring us down and attack our place of security.

When we remain in the place of strength and security and our trust is in the Lord, the invading forces and galley ships or war and destruction will not be able to penetrate our defenses, they cannot dwell where the majestic presence of the Lord rules.

I believe *verse 23* is talking about how the enemies power is taken off him and he is unable to penetrate where Gods presence rules.
Even the lame who takes hold of the Lord in his heart will be able to take plunder back from the enemy. Next we get to the part that says no one will say *"I am sick"* now that is freedom and liberty and a place of wholeness, confidence in the promises of God.

Now the connector once again, the people who dwell in the place of security will be forgiven of their iniquity and find healing.

Even when we are lame and the enemy seems to have tight grip on our lives and he keeps sending battle ships our way, if we come to the place of taking hold of God and His Kingdom then we will be forgiven and when we are in that place, sickness has no right to be there.

Psalm 107:42
42 The righteous see it and rejoice
And all iniquity stops its mouth.

This is powerful and liberating! The Throne of Iniquity who accuse by the law must stop their mouth in the face of Jesus Christ who is Lord above all.

The righteous, that is us when we are in His Kingdom, will see this great freedom and rejoice with grateful hearts.

How does God respond to the taunts and accusations of the enemy against us?

Zechariah 3:2-4
2 And the LORD said to Satan, "The LORD rebuke you, Satan! The LORD who has chosen Jerusalem rebuke you! Is this not a brand plucked from the fire?"
3 Now Joshua was clothed with filthy garments, and was standing before the Angel.
4 Then He answered and spoke to those who stood before Him, saying, "Take away the filthy garments from him." And to him He said, "See, I have removed your iniquity from you, and I will clothe you with rich robes."

That is Gods heart towards you and me and all of mankind, He wants to rebuke the enemy on our behalf and all iniquity must be silenced when God says my Son Jesus has taken the sin of mankind upon Himself and canceled the law of accusation that was against us due to sin.

He has removed the power of iniquity from us and we don't have to be under its rule and influence anymore, we can transfer our fellowship and thinking into the Kingdom of God and find the fellowship we have been longing for that will bring freedom to our souls.

There is an Abundance of Grace given to Rule and Reign above the Control of the evil one. The gift of righteousness provides the position legally to rule and reign by the blood of Jesus.

We either rule and reign above the circumstances as co-heirs with Christ or we become subject to our circumstances by the influence of the dominions of darkness.
Establish and build your steps from the perspective of being positioned above where we rule and reign.
Speak the word of faith, as the place that is established for us is in Christ.

Call things that are not as though they are – as a faith statement for your life.
What if we feel we just cannot change, our hearts have been so dominated by the powers of darkness, they bring us all the way down, we are goners and we just don't know any other way?

God can do anything, but what about changing the heart if willing?

Psalm 51:10-13
10 Create in me a clean heart, O God,
And renew a steadfast spirit within me.
11 Do not cast me away from Your presence,
And do not take Your Holy Spirit from me.
12 Restore to me the joy of Your salvation,
And uphold me by Your generous Spirit.
13 Then I will teach transgressors Your ways,
And sinners shall be converted to You.

"Create in me a clean heart" can be our prayer.
"Renew a steadfast and right spirit within me" can be something we can see developed in our life as we call out to God for His ability and help to get us through.

We are a new creation, that is how God sees us, we might not be there yet and have a lot of work to be done to bring us to the place of confidence. When we have had a lifetime of being under it and living in dark ways it is ingrained into our character and mindset. But just as God removed the iniquity from Joshua the High priest and changed his clothes from filth to righteousness and gave him a whole new way of thinking, He will do the same for us. Just keep standing on what God says and not how it seems, a seed when it is planted takes time to grow into a mature and fruitful plant, if we persist and remain in fellowship it will come, sometimes fast growth sometimes gradual, He is faithful and His love will never fail to change your life from out of the ash heap to righteousness and peace.

In the Old Testament they were looking forward to the promise of a Saviour and asked for the transformation based on what will happen.
In the New Testament we are a new creation and it has already been done for us looking back to the finished work of the cross, so we can receive what is already provided.

We align with the truth. We receive by faith of the New Life.

We can declare in faith that we have a clean heart and a steadfast and new spirit. **"I am a new creation"**

It appears that the provision of the cross and the abundance of Gods grace covers every place of weakness and lack in our lives and is able to raise us up from the dead state, to being transformed by His glorious light. Remember Lazarus he was in the tomb, dead until Jesus came, Abraham had no hope to have a child as his body was as good as dead. Moses had no confidence to lead or speak until God came with ability and power from above which is above the place of defeat and failure. God in His mercy will not leave us in a state of weakness which brings hopelessness in a continual place of defeat; No He came to give us victory.

Psalm 51:1, 2
Have mercy upon me, O God,
According to Your lovingkindness;
According to the multitude of Your tender mercies,
Blot out my transgressions.
2 Wash me thoroughly from my iniquity,
And cleanse me from my sin.

According to Gods loving kindness and the multitude of tender mercies we are set free. That's the place we would rather be where we receive His endless love.

- *Removal - Blot out - transgressions – are acts.*
- *Process - Wash me thoroughly – iniquity is an embedded sinful state.*
- *Process - Cleanse me - sin is the inherent ability to do wrong.*

He has many ways to deal with the issue of sin in our lives, there are times of washing and inner cleansing as well as blotting out from the issues that accuse us and tell us that we are no good, rotten and filthy sinners.
We can yield to His process and the dealings that will bring the changes that we cry out for, to be truly free.

Psalm 32:1-5
Blessed is he whose transgression is forgiven,
Whose sin is covered.
2 Blessed is the man to whom the LORD does not impute iniquity,
And in whose spirit there is no deceit.
3 When I kept silent, my bones grew old Through my groaning all the day long.
4 For day and night Your hand was heavy upon me;
My vitality was turned into the drought of summer. Selah
5 I acknowledged my sin to You,
And my iniquity I have not hidden.
I said, "I will confess my transgressions to the LORD,"
And You forgave the iniquity of my sin.
Selah

Acknowledgement of your sins is the first step and the right way to go and allow God to deal with all of the aspects of forgiveness and cleansing your conscience, so that you can walk in the blessings of God and have the heavy weights removed from your life.

Psalm 107:19, 20
19 Then they cried out to the LORD in their trouble,
And He saved them out of their distresses.
20 He sent His word and healed them,
And delivered them from their destructions.

God will save you from trouble when you cry out to Him, His love is there always waiting for us to come to His place of security.
He will send His word of healing, yes one word from God will deliver us from our destructive ways, we just need to receive it and place ourselves where His presence and grace can bring strong deliverance to our every circumstance. Our circumstances maybe a direct result of our actions that a lifestyle of iniquity had placed us under, most likely it is, Jesus places us above and delivers us from all of the affects of sin.

Allow the Love of the Father to permeate the temple which is in your body where your heart and soul lives and receive the abundance.

1 John 3:1-3
Behold what manner of love the Father has bestowed on us, that we should be called children of God!
Therefore the world does not know us, because it did not know Him.
2 Beloved, now we are children of God; and it has not yet been revealed what we shall be, but we know that when He is revealed, we shall be like Him, for we shall see Him as He is.
3 And everyone who has this hope in Him purifies himself, just as He is pure.

We are accepted and loved by the Father and He has provided the very best for our lives. We are His children and we have access to all that He has and His DNA flows through us in a new and living way. We can activate what belongs to us by faith and take hold of the life that will take us into the higher realm of the Father that the world does not comprehend.

We overcome.

CHAPTER 7

Light Love and Peace

Light, Love and Peace these are Heavens Vibe Man!!!
Is it possible for a bright light to come and light up your life?
Sometimes when we experience times of trouble, the bright sunshine of vibrancy for our life is obscured by big black clouds of gloom.

If you experienced love and acceptance like never before from the God who holds all of the universe together, would your peace level get a boost and would you be lifted up to the bright and the light clouds which are resting way above your darkest troubles?

I would like to give you my testimony, which is my first experience of knowing God and receiving a life changing encounter from God. This occurred in my early teens, I was someone who had no belief in God that became transformed into a believer by the Holy Sprint who came and in an instant, filled my entire being with *Light, Love and Peace.* Man Alive!

A simple prayer was made *"ask the Holy Spirit to come"* and this was the early 1970's in a Lutheran Church located in a rural city in Australia.

So it was a radical prayer for the time, it came from a visiting speaker for a youth meeting, it is possible that the speaker had witnessed Kathryn Kuhlman or experienced the Jesus Movement of that time.

The experience began with the sense that a light unlike any light I had ever known with a brilliant intensity filling my being, followed by receiving the love of God, which was a love far above anything I had ever known and with it came the knowing that Jesus died for my sins and I knew that God loved me, lastly I was filled by a sense of a tangible peace within, which again was far above and unlike anything I had ever experienced before.

So what I received was, firstly the Light that came into my being like an energy force that seemed to be coming from the centre of my heart and seemed to fill my entire body; next I felt the Love of God that totally overwhelmed me and with it came, in an instant; the knowledge of what Jesus did for me on the cross which was followed by the Peace that totally put my mind at ease.

I was a young teenager that never knew God or believed in Him at all, and I was permitted to have an encounter with the living presence of God that was profound and life changing, my belief and thinking was transformed forever.

I received a faith and a knowing that God was real and that He loved me and Jesus had died for my sins. God turned my world upside down by a filling of His Presence which comes by the Holy Spirit and I received a knowing that was beyond my intellect and my perception of reality.

When I was a young person I had an appreciation for art and the sciences and I was impressed by people of history such as Leonardo Da Vinci from the Renaissance period, I greatly admired his inventive intelligence and creative abilities.

However, the experience of the encounter with God made a lasting impression that introduced me to a whole new level of understanding, beyond what I could have known and God will take us out of what we perceive in the natural; we enter into the higher world of the spirit realm, this hidden dimension of the spirit actually holds our world together, from a higher place and operates on higher laws that contain all of the laws of our known physical world.

Back in the heyday of the 60's flower and peace movement there was a lot of talk about getting set free from the establishment that held people down and put them in a box, it was all about finding harmony and peace and there also was a lot of talk about love.

Lonnie Frisbee was an evangelist of the 60's Jesus Revival movement who was a hippie type person and he represented something new and radical, and he wasn't part of the establishment.
Lonnie identified with the peace movement and brought in a radical and revolutionary Good News about Jesus and the Love of God. There were many young people that were saved during these times and they were all looking for something that was about peace and love, which was free from the corruption and the machinery of the system of society, they identified with real people that were instrumental in liberating them.

When I first encountered God, He gave me True Love and Peace and also, the Light that was above any energy of this world.
I have come to understand that the Light is like the life energy substance of God, that is like pure power and heavenly matter from above and the Peace of God is like being in the zone or the good vibrations of Heaven, Peace is the Security of Heaven that everything will be alright man, these energies and frequencies are the vibes you feel and sense when you are in the Love of God.
However, this does not by any means explain or provide a full understanding of the life of God from a higher dimension, this is only a glimpse from my human perspective, a misty bit of revelation of the splendour of God's wonders.

You can't separate the energy and vibrations of Heaven from His person, He is Jesus the Son of God, He is Love, Love is who He is and what He does.
The energy from God is full of His love and life and the character of God and His peace has a similar sense about it. The light is a glowing light with the vibrant brightness of all the colours of Heaven, like a rainbow and His peace carries with it the feelings of a place of real security, with a vibration that lifts your spirit and fills you with a wind of refreshing.

Knowing the principles of how this world functions and knowledge of the laws of science with some complex formulas thrown in won't give you peace, the light bulb might go on, but it won't compare to the filling knowledge of the brightness of Gods brilliant light.

The light and peace from God can be perceived in many more facets and expressions than our perceptions of natural light and feelings of peace.
So there are higher laws that operate in the spirit world that are above the natural laws of our physical world and these higher laws hold and govern the natural world we live in.

John 1:1-5
In the beginning was the Word, and the Word was with God, and the Word was God.
2 He was in the beginning with God.

3 All things were made through Him, and without Him nothing was made that was made.
4 In Him was life, and the life was the light of men.
5 And the light shines in the darkness, and the darkness did not comprehend it.

Jesus was the Word of God and He made everything, He is our life and this life is the light or our energy that sustains us.
This light is evident but we do not comprehend it, the scientists are still baffled about what mysterious energy holds atoms together and gives substance to matter.

We kind of know something is there, there is some type of life or force that works in all things but we don't really see or know what it is.

John 1:9
9 That was the true Light which gives light to every man coming into the world.

There is a truth to all things and the something that makes us tick. There is a true light that goes on inside us and without it we are black empty matter.

Hebrews 1:1-3
God, who at various times and in various ways spoke in time past to the fathers by the prophets,

2 has in these last days spoken to us by His Son, whom He has appointed heir of all things, through whom also He made the worlds;
3 who being the brightness of His glory and the express image of His person, and upholding all things by the word of His power, when He had by Himself purged our sins, sat down at the right hand of the Majesty on high.

We need to be connected to the source of our life, this is the true light and Jesus is the expression of the light and energy of God, it is no wonder that He is able to deal with our disconnection by sin and plug us back into the brightness of the light of life.

Light and Peace are perceived and felt by our human spirit, which is our connector to the power source and life from above and all things are held together by His Word. Without the light we lose our life, however, even objects that are inanimate like a block of wood is made up of atoms and molecules and they have a life that is spinning and vibrating.

John 14:25-27
25 "These things I have spoken to you while being present with you.
26 But the Helper, the Holy Spirit, whom the Father will send in My name, He will teach you all things, and bring to your remembrance all things that I said to you.

27 Peace I leave with you, My peace I give to you; not as the world gives do I give to you. Let not your heart be troubled, neither let it be afraid.

When we become believers and give our lives to our Lord Jesus Christ, the Holy Spirit comes into our beings and He brings the Presence and Glory of God. We receive the Truth and reality of God, the Holy Spirit is Gods Spirit who is with us on earth and when He comes He is Light and He is Peace, the characteristics of God are felt and seen by our spirit connection and sometimes His Presence can also be perceived in our natural environment.

When we allow the Holy Spirit sent from God to come and give us what is from above, this takes us beyond the limitations of our worldly knowledge of the physical environment to a higher dimension, this is where we can learn to walk in the flow of life from a higher place, above the hindrance of fear and anxiety of how to deal with life and the trouble in this world. Jesus has given us His peace for the here and now for our present situation and this is a peace that world cannot give in turmoil and confusion.

Jesus does not give as the world gives, as the world can only offer a limited knowledge and understanding to deal with the issues that we face.

The world has developed knowledge in psychology, sciences and technology and there is much expertise that can help us with the troubles of this world, but when we connect with the source of life who is Jesus, His peace brings us above the human perceived levels of knowledge of our world.

Jesus came from above and He knew how to operate in this world and also the hidden world of the spirit and that enabled Him to keep in perfect peace.

He did not succumb to the pressures and the opposing crowds of society, He moved in a different way, that allowed Him to glide through trouble and He could see in the Spirit to enable Him to deal with the hidden forces that may try to pull Him back down.

The world does have a type of peace that it can give, but only like a prescription drug it can dull the pain, but it doesn't cure the root of the problem.

The worlds solutions and methods for our peace all have their value, but as we can see, in a world that daily is shocked and plagued by a lot of bad news headlines, about out of control people getting into strife and conflict, the world cannot fix itself with the tools and the tricks of the humanistic trades.

Why do we pursue peace? Our soul desperately needs peace, when we are in a constant state of processing information and the input is increasingly negative and draining, it creates a stress which is overwhelming, we need to return to a place of equilibrium or a place of rest that restores a healthy state of being.

The instruction of Jesus is -
"Let not your heart become troubled".
"Neither let it be afraid".

This world's trouble brings fear, there is bad news, adverse circumstances and there is a mood of distress.
These forces oppose our peace and the thought of them can take away our peace if we let it.

When trouble comes our minds may be hustled away from the good things of life and our focus will be on the circumstances we find ourselves in.
The Good News is that Peace comes from within us.

We have the ability to shift our focus and find the peace that will sustain us through troubled times.
Philippians 4:6-8
6 Be anxious for nothing, but in everything by prayer and supplication, with thanksgiving, let your requests be made known to God;

7 and the peace of God, which surpasses all understanding, will guard your hearts and minds through Christ Jesus.
8 Finally, brethren, whatever things are true, whatever things are noble, whatever things are just, whatever things are pure, whatever things are lovely, whatever things are of good report, if there is any virtue and if there is anything praiseworthy—meditate on these things.

There is a knowing that can come that is from above, it passes all of our known understanding and takes us above the problem into a whole new light.
There can be a knowing that you have it and it will work out for the good.
We can see this represented by a diagram, our thinking level comparison.

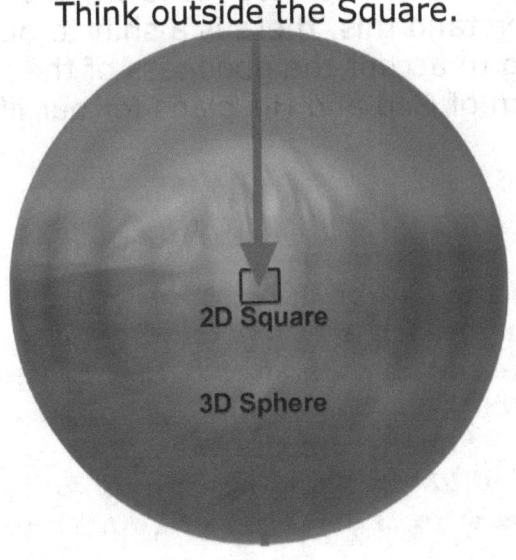

Peace passes our understanding so when we do what we naturally try to do; solve our problems and figure it all out by applying the knowledge that we know and things still don't change or get worse this sends us into depression and frustration. Nothing seems to work out and there is no peace in that.
Gods peace is above our natural understanding and we need to tune into the sound and vibration that is from above, the Word of God brings light to our understanding which will allow us to see the higher order of things that is above our circumstances and when we know the love of God and His acceptance, we can trust that He can turn things around for our good and move the negative forces into submission by the higher energy of God.

There are higher laws that can kick in for our good and not for our harm and when we begin to understand this, there is a shift to our thinking to accept the goodness of the Kingdom of God and His plans for our life.

Psalm 61:1-4
Hear my cry, O God;
Attend to my prayer.
2 From the end of the earth I will cry to You,
When my heart is overwhelmed;
Lead me to the rock that is higher than I.
3 For You have been a shelter for me,
A strong tower from the enemy.
4 I will abide in Your tabernacle forever;
I will trust in the shelter of Your wings.

When you are overwhelmed by life's problems and your inability to deal with them, you can cry out to God who leads you to the higher place where His peace rules and you will see His protection in a strong tower and shelter from the negative forces that may have come against you.

Proverbs 4:20-23
20 My son, give attention to my words;
Incline your ear to my sayings.
21 Do not let them depart from your eyes;
Keep them in the midst of your heart;
22 For they are life to those who find them,
23 Keep your heart with all diligence,
For out of it spring the issues of life.

We have a choice in how we deal with what is in our hearts and minds and what we allow to dominate our thinking, if we allow negative thoughts and the weight and oppression of our circumstances to occupy our minds, we will be subject to its consequences. Or we can take His Word and Promises and meditate and speak the blessings of God over our life and His will is done on earth for our lives.

We can see the light of Gods Good plans for us and the light has an energy and power with it to create the breakthrough for your life. Anxiety will keep you in a state of hopelessness and there is no peace in that mode, your heart and mind are out of synch with the good vibration of Heaven.

When you shift your thinking and keep the word of God in your heart, this will shift your focus to the security of the love and promises of God.

The peace of God is your guard, it is the shelter and a place of being in a strong tower where you can switch onto Gods frequency, His life will spring forth from your heart that no longer is overtaken by anxiety.

God is our security in this world, there is no other security that compares to what God offers, as His security is from a Higher Place and this place can be built on this earth.

Isaiah 26:1-6

"We have a strong city;
God will appoint salvation for walls and bulwarks.
2 Open the gates,
That the righteous nation which keeps the truth may enter in.
3 You will keep him in perfect peace,
Whose mind is stayed on You,
Because he trusts in You.
4 Trust in the LORD forever,
For in YAH, the LORD, is everlasting strength.
5 For He brings down those who dwell on high,
The lofty city;
He lays it low,
He lays it low to the ground,
He brings it down to the dust.
6 The foot shall tread it down—
The feet of the poor
And the steps of the needy."

There is much unrest and dissatisfaction for the establishment today, as many governments and authorities and especially harsh dictators, are being challenged by the masses in many protests on the streets. There is an awakening to the fact that the greedy elements of the global world of dominating companies of the mega rich are controlling the masses and there is an imbalance; as the costs of living are increasing and we the average people barely manage to survive. Conspiracy theories abound with most of the profits of the current increasing costs are going to the dominating few, there is corruption and even the way money is controlled seems to be out of control and based on getting the masses into debt, which is oppressive and based in greed.

John 14:1
"Let not your heart be troubled; you believe in God, believe also in Me.
Believing in Jesus is the key to letting not your heart to be weighed down.
Peace is knowing that you are loved and that your trust is in the Higher Authority, that is above the circumstances of life that will try to rob you of your God given peace.
Faith holds on to what is ours and belongs to us in Christ.

The world offers security by its own resources and it is conditional and unreliable, depending on whether it suits its own purposes at that time.

The worlds solutions can be well meaning, but they are not dependable and subject to change.

Depending on the Government to solve all of our problems – to offer a health and welfare system to look after us is not the answer for our future, I think those funds are shaky and spent on the pressures of massive debts.

Peace that is above our understanding and knowledge,
"passes all understanding"
which is another level and another frequency that we can tune into.
It is a knowing that God will come through with His promises.
Like faith, it is being in the *ZONE* or the feels *'just right'* place.
Our soul processes and receives knowledge, this can be good or it can be bad depending on what is received.

Our heart is who we are and what we believe, so we need to guard carefully what can keep us in a place of security when all has turned to custard.

Tune into the frequency of Heaven and be a Believer Receiver.
Tune away from the bombardment of background noise of confusion, static and alternative frequencies.

On the Radio – our radio – what we are tuned into – make it crystal clear.

Move away from the interference and the hiss of noise that is on the wrong channels and tune into the good vibrations of Gods wonderful Peace that the world cannot ever give.

Ephesians 3:14-21
14 For this reason I bow my knees to the Father of our Lord Jesus Christ,
15 from whom the whole family in heaven and earth is named,
16 that He would grant you, according to the riches of His glory, to be strengthened with might through His Spirit in the inner man,
17 that Christ may dwell in your hearts through faith; that you, being rooted and grounded in love,
18 may be able to comprehend with all the saints what is the width and length and depth and height—
19 to know the love of Christ which passes knowledge; that you may be filled with all the fullness of God.
20 Now to Him who is able to do exceedingly abundantly above all that we ask or think, according to the power that works in us,
21 to Him be glory in the church by Christ Jesus to all generations, forever and ever. Amen.

The Holy Spirit fills the temple of our body and the whole person –
mind, intellect, emotions, as He connects to the spirit man.
There is a love that passes knowledge, as our knowledge is not the same as the experience of receiving the love of God that He liberally gives to us personally.
Love cannot be computed by a thought process and calculated into a theory or formula. Love is felt and experienced in our hearts and this love does not come from only knowledge gained from intensive study of the scriptures and religious books, true love can only come from knowing and being with our God.
He is always there reaching out to us to receive it, it is up to us to respond and enter into a higher place of knowing Him and His love that will give us peace and fill us up with a confidence that can face the storms of life and our personal issues.

Mark 4:35-41
35 On the same day, when evening had come, He said to them, "Let us cross over to the other side."
36 Now when they had left the multitude, they took Him along in the boat as He was. And other little boats were also with Him.
37 And a great windstorm arose, and the waves beat into the boat, so that it was already filling.
38 But He was in the stern, asleep on a pillow. And they awoke Him and said to Him, "Teacher, do You not care that we are perishing?"

39 Then He arose and rebuked the wind, and said to the sea, "Peace, be still!" And the wind ceased and there was a great calm.
40 But He said to them, "Why are you so fearful? How is it that you have no faith?"
41 And they feared exceedingly, and said to one another, "Who can this be, that even the wind and the sea obey Him!"

Jesus moved and was tuned into the vibrations of Heaven and when He commanded the storm which was confronting in the natural environment; it had to obey Him and His words and conform to the frequency of Heaven which was peace and be still.

Storms and adverse winds are unrest and excessive activity that are beyond the normal operation of smooth sailing and they prevent us from getting to our destination in safety.

Jesus is in tune with the Holy Spirit, He was filled without measure, He had the harmony and authority of Heaven and He simply released the positive energy of peace into the negative energy of the contrary winds of the storm and neutralized it, the chaotic opposition had to obey and be still and conform to the good vibration of peace.

Psalm 107:23-31
23 Those who go down to the sea in ships,
Who do business on great waters,
24 They see the works of the LORD,
And His wonders in the deep.

25 For He commands and raises the stormy wind,
Which lifts up the waves of the sea.
26 They mount up to the heavens,
They go down again to the depths;
Their soul melts because of trouble.
27 They reel to and fro, and stagger like a drunken man,
And are at their wits' end.
28 Then they cry out to the LORD in their trouble,
And He brings them out of their distresses.
29 He calms the storm,
So that its waves are still.
30 Then they are glad because they are quiet;
So He guides them to their desired haven.
31 Oh, that men would give thanks to the LORD for His goodness,
And for His wonderful works to the children of men!

We all face adversity and the storms of life are like facing opposition.

God has permitted conditions and effects to come and there are physical laws and higher laws that create atmosphere and movement a certain way by a cause. We have been given the right to have dominion and to learn what it is to overcome, as we live by faith and not by sight we can grow in ability and be able to master the opposition that we face.

You see there are wonders in the deep and the deep is below the surface, it is something that operates on another hidden level, but it is the part that governs what happens in the visible. So what we see is not the workings and the operation of all the layers of the dimensions, it is the material visual presentation only. We are not dealing with what is visible only, in the storms that come and they are very fierce and adverse which can rob us of what? Our peace and this will take us out of faith and into fear, and then our enemy has access to control our circumstances using the visible adverse conditions.

What God is saying is that He created the physical laws that govern storms which allow them to come into being from a source, so the storm that was commanded by Jesus to be still was out of order, the physical properties that made the storm needed to be ordered back into peace. God has made the elements and the energy lows and highs and the laws of physics which operate on our visual plane of physical earth, but there is also spiritual laws operating that are hidden in the deep, like the laws of quantum physics and the universal spiritual laws that are working above and govern our natural laws.
These spiritual laws were all created by God for us to learn and be Co-Heirs with Jesus, to rule and reign and be above and be the ruler over the opposition and things that are not Gods will for us.

Left to our own strength and our own limited knowledge without God's light, we will come to our wits end and believe me when that happens, there is no peace in life, but a lot of anxiety, stress and frustration.

That is why peace is such an important element for our life, because it places us into a different place of dealing with life's storms and this is when we step up into the God Zone or the place where Jesus rules from.

Jesus is our Head and our Lord, He is the one we look up to and find truth and the battle plans to overcome.

Jesus challenged the disciples saying *"where is your faith!"* He was saying to them you can do something about it and you can deal with this and then demonstrated to them how it is done and Jesus was a man as well as God, so that is why He is our example to follow.
He can lead us to a desired haven and that is a safe place of security where we are on track with God in our lives, in a place where we are connected to Him and His resources, to be successful in business as well as our occupations and our calling in life.

Perhaps if we are in a constant storm in life it is because there are some adjustments needed to get us back to the desired place, whether it is a literal move or a shift in our thinking to align with Gods ways.

If God is the creator of all of these laws that create the storms and the winds, then He actually is above all of those laws and has complete control over them. They are not going to get out of hand even by the fiercest devil out there, so Jesus as a man submitted to His Father only had to connect with the moving of His Spirit and command peace and the winds and the storm to be still.

Sometimes all of the noise and the din of life gets out of hand and reaches a dominating level that wants to override our peace, we need to stay tuned into what God is doing and saying.

That's when we need to get still before Him and tune into His frequency and the waves of peace and find our authority over the storm, we can command our situation to be at peace. First we need to be in a place that is desirable by God where our hearts and minds are tuned into what the Spirit is saying and where He leads us, in that place of great peace, the gift of faith will flow easily and we will be Gods voice to move things into the right perspective.

The winds and waves of life that are out of control and oppose our destiny will obey the command of Heaven which is Peace.
Tune in, do not be fearful, don't let your heart be afraid or troubled find the peace of God and release it into the circumstances that prevents your boat from arriving.

Be in faith – believe in Jesus not in the circumstances of the storm that comes in ferociousness and lots of noise and clamor.

What are our instruments and dials, when we are driving along and on the road of life? We need these instruments in our vehicle to warn us when things need attention and maintenance and there are also signs on the road that point us to our destination safely. Lack of Peace is imbalance with the harmonics and frequency of Heaven and can be perceived in your spirit as a wrong sound or vibration that is out of sequence with what is known as peace, or the right frequency of Peace.

Sometimes we need to get into the place where we are still from life's distractions and noise and come before God in His presence. We can switch onto His frequency of peace where all of the noise and clamour, won't interfere and overwhelm.

It can be a real place of rest in God, just what we need to get us through the tough times and the rough part of the journey.

1 Peter 5:6-9
6 Therefore humble yourselves under the mighty hand of God, that He may exalt you in due time,
7 casting all your care upon Him, for He cares for you.

8 Be sober, be vigilant; because your adversary the devil walks about like a roaring lion, seeking whom he may devour. 9 Resist him, steadfast in the faith, knowing that the same sufferings are experienced by your brotherhood in the world.

Not being anxious and not letting our hearts being troubled can also mean to unload the heavy cares that will weigh upon us, as these are just too much for us to deal with on our own. We can resist the opposition and remain steady in faith in Jesus and what He has provided for us to walk in and have peace in this world.

Isaiah 66:12, 13
12 For thus says the LORD:
"Behold, I will extend peace to her like a river,
And the glory of the Gentiles like a flowing stream.
Then you shall feed;
On her sides shall you be carried,
And be dandled on her knees.
13 As one whom his mother comforts,
So I will comfort you;
And you shall be comforted in Jerusalem."

Sometimes you just gotta jump in, when you are all hot and bothered what is the remedy? Find that river that is pure and flowing in the gentle, soothing, stream of peace. We just need to get into the flow like the river.

Psalm 36:7-9
7 How precious is Your lovingkindness, O God!
Therefore the children of men put their trust under the shadow of Your wings.
8 They are abundantly satisfied with the fullness of Your house,
And You give them drink from the river of Your pleasures.
9 For with You is the fountain of life;
In Your light we see light.

When you get into the flow of life and the source of life, you just drink in the goodness and it fills your whole being.
What a place to be, abundantly filled, satisfied by Gods fullness, God just wants us to drink this in, we need to tap into the fountain of life that is freely offered and we need to actively receive what we have been given by the loving kindness of God. When we come to a place of seeing this liberating and wonderful truth, it is a light, this light goes on inside us and we truly light up.

Come on then man, this is the real thing! A fountain is a living, vibrating, magnificent flow of living water, the sustenance of life surging through our being will cause us to take off in life like never before.

Can I say *Wow Man!!!* Just like the 60's Peace Movement, I would like to use that language here again, like wow man, Gods Love Rules!!!

This is the peace movement like never before and God has so much for us to take hold of, that is full of life and light that is a real pleasure.

Colossians 3:14-17
14 But above all these things put on love, which is the bond of perfection.
15 And let the peace of God rule in your hearts, to which also you were called in one body; and be thankful.
16 Let the word of Christ dwell in you richly in all wisdom, teaching and admonishing one another in psalms and hymns and spiritual songs, singing with grace in your hearts to the Lord.
17 And whatever you do in word or deed, do all in the name of the Lord Jesus, giving thanks to God the Father through Him.

It all comes back to love and being in the love, a bit like the river you can jump into that and drink from the fountain, it is Gods love that we can have and move in.

This is revolution, world changing peace and love not war, type of language and it is all possible, because with God it is all possible. Once again we have the instruction to let the peace of God rule in our hearts, it is something we allow and cultivate, so it is being switched on as opposed to off.
Like when they say *"he is off"* be a right on brother and a right on sister in the love of God and let that peace rule above.

His word illuminates the truth of His love and guides our understanding and we can rule with His peace governing our hearts, where the fountain springs up in songs of thanking God for all of these blessings.

There is a peace and a love that we can have that is just like Jesus, when He lived and moved on this earth, He invites us to partake of the same.

Like as in the resurrection life that Jesus provided, we can rise up with peace that is above our understanding.

1 John 4:17
17 Love has been perfected among us in this: that we may have boldness in the day of judgment;
because as He is, so are we in this world.

We are on His wavelength above natural knowledge and understanding, birthed into a higher frequency.

1 John 1:7
7 But if we walk in the light as He is in the light, we have fellowship with one another, and the blood of Jesus Christ His Son cleanses us from all sin.

We can walk as He walked, since He has given us of the light of His love and the peace that is above, so that we can rise above the knocks of life to a flow and a moving that is in step with Him.

Lets go on the Peace program with Jesus as our guide and teacher and He will show us how to walk – we glide with the skill of Heaven and right through where there is much noise and the knocks from the hustle and bustle that life throws at us.

The good thing is that Gods love and His light and peace are tangible and they can be experienced in our lives. They are not just concepts or knowledge that we gain like a feather in our cap, but we can experience the reality of God's love and His goodness, as it fills our lives in a spectrum of light and colour and the vibe of peace.

So there is a contrast from when we operate outside and separate to God to when we are with Him and partnering with Him and His Kingdom.

LIGHT – DARK.

Romans 8:6-8
6 For to be carnally minded is death, but to be spiritually minded is life and peace.
7 Because the carnal mind is enmity against God; for it is not subject to the law of God, nor indeed can be.
8 So then, those who are in the flesh cannot please God.

In the flesh we cannot please God.

When our mind has been tuned in and tuned to run smoothly on good oil we are on the right frequency and the tune we play is good, not with discord that is out of harmony with the peace of God.

Romans 8:9, 10
9 But you are not in the flesh but in the Spirit, if indeed the Spirit of God dwells in you. Now if anyone does not have the Spirit of Christ, he is not His.
10 And if Christ is in you, the body is dead because of sin, but the Spirit is life because of righteousness.

Now when we are in Christ and we are His, our spirit is alive, switched on, activated to be in tune and operate with God and the result is life and peace.

Romans 8:11
11 But if the Spirit of Him who raised Jesus from the dead dwells in you, He who raised Christ from the dead will also give life to your mortal bodies through His Spirit who dwells in you.

This is the life that the Holy Spirit brings and we can see it is resurrection life that is transferred from our spirit into our bodies which is the temple of the Holy Spirit.
Moses had some type of glory in the form of light in his body that was visible, after He was with God on the mountain for 40 days and 40 nights.

Jesus was transfigured and shone like the brightest light when He was on earth in His earthly body as a man.

The glory that Moses had was old covenant and we are in the times of the new covenant, which is a new and living way that brings liberation from being under the law that brings death because of sin.
Lazarus received resurrection life and he was raised from the dead, his mortal body was reactivated and restored by the living power of God.

Abraham considered that his body was as good as dead to conceive the promised child, but he was strengthened by faith in what God had promised and received a miracle in his body. This is what is available to us today as believers, the living power of God that can transform us into a whole new creation, as that is who we are in the resurrection life of Christ. Our spirit is alive because of righteousness, we are now under the grace offered by Jesus and His blood covers us, to provide a right standing with God and so now we are positioned to receive His resurrection life, which is the light of life that empowers our physical bodies.

The higher law now operates to activate the lower properties of our material substance, as now our spirit is plugged into the source of energy from above.

His light will bring power and life to our beings and reveal truth, so that we can see that we have the security of Heaven and this brings great peace to our hearts where previously, we lived in fear of the forces that bring the consequences that eventually leads to death.
Romans 8:13, 14
13 For if you live according to the flesh you will die; but if by the Spirit you put to death the deeds of the body, you will live.
14 For as many as are led by the Spirit of God, these are sons of God.
How we are led can be a tangible experience that we can have and develop when we grow up in the knowledge and our relationship with Him.
It is learning to flow in the spirit, there is peace and we know His love is a motivation, there is a light that comes on when we move this way, our spirit is alive to the things of the spirit and we can develop and grow as we partake and activate what is ours as sons of God, we are related to Him and are plugged into His life to be and do all we can be in Christ, as we walk in the light as He is the light.
Praying in the Spirit also switches us on and plugs us directly into the source of energy for walking the plan of God for our lives, when we bypass our limitation of natural thinking and connect with the power source that is above our understanding, we are tuned in to Gods wavelength without the distractions of our fears and what we see in our circumstances.

The misdeeds of the flesh and our carnal behaviors will produce death and we can sense a bad vibration of a lack of peace and a lack of His life, which results in a darkness overshadowing our lives and I think that we can perceive this feeling and know when our hearts are troubled by the wrong motivations of our carnal appetites.

Rom 8:24-25
24 For we were saved in this hope, but hope that is seen is not hope; for why does one still hope for what he sees?
25 But if we hope for what we do not see, we eagerly wait for it with perseverance.

Growing up is a process, and learning is an exercise of finding our way, it is OK to miss the way when you a learner,
we can just get up again and keep walking until it comes right and it will as God is our Father and His love is big enough to handle our growth wobbles and help us on our way.
The carnal man is driven by fleshly appetites of lust that cannot be satisfied.
The spirit man is energized by the light and frequency from above.
These are the higher levels laws and since we are now switched on we can learn these ways.

Jesus walked on the water by the laws that are above.

They thought He was a ghost – they perceived He was different than the normal bloke and had some ability that was out of this world.
It was a light energy from above and it became visible to men and perceived by the spirit.

Peter walked on the water by faith, so he was invited by Jesus and He walked as Jesus walked.
Walk in the Light as He is the Light is the invite.
Speak peace and still the waves of the world that are contrary, there are waves of the storm of the world, so keep your eyes on Jesus who is above those waves.

Experience the tangible reality of the substance of Heaven – the Energy of Life, Light, Peace, Love.

Jesus walked and moved on another plane - one that wasn't restricted by the constraints and the pressures of our world. He walked on the water.
Jesus walked on the water – above and He was a Being in the Light.
Jesus commanded "*Peace! Be Still*!" to the environment and the atmosphere and the mood of the situation.
The worldly elements must obey the higher laws and conform to the order and vibration as in Heaven let it be on earth, peace and be still.

Walk in the light as He is in the light.

The presence of the Holy Spirit brings Gods light, Jesus lived in the Spirit of God, He was filled with the Spirit without measure.
Jesus flowed with the Spirit and He moved with the Spirit, He had great peace as the circumstances and opposition that this world brings is below the power of the light and glory of God and must obey and come under the authority that Gods Power on earth brings.

The peace is above our understanding and the love of God surpasses knowledge. If we could activate the power of God on information alone there would be a lot of cosmic cowboy Christians shooting the place up with lasers.

When we mature we are trusted with and can handle more authority, moving with the Love of God and the Spirit of God is when the power kicks in, as this is the connection to the light into our beings. We are either a being who is out of tune with God or we are a *"Being in the Light"*, in tune with God which brings a sense of peace into our lives.

Final Note on experience:

Faith is not based on experience alone; our faith is based always on the truth of His Word. We cant expect that there will always be a supernatural mind blowing experience to lead us all of the way, perceiving His peace can be very still and quiet, like a whisper, peace may not be very loud and evident, compared to all of the sensory noises and sights around us.

Sometimes it is preferable for us not to depend on experience alone, but a trust that grows from our personal relationship with God. We live by faith and not by sight and so we are led by what is perceived in our spirit and not by an experience. The experience is part of the whole and it is something that we cannot manufacture or conjure up, when it comes, it comes and it is a wonderful part of the interaction with the spiritual realm.

Can we ask God for more? I believe by all means yes, desire it and give Him permission to show you great and wonderful things that you know not.

Also, the experience I had will not be the same for you and that is why we can't compare our experience to someone else, as He will lead each of us in an individual way.

On the other hand if all we know is the knowledge of the Word without really knowing Him, or experiencing His love in some way other than gaining information, then this is a very academic Christianity, which I feel is lacking as God made us with all of our senses to experience life and I am sure that He can be experienced in much greater ways than the interaction we have with His creation and the material world.

This is new ground for me and a place of discovery as I venture out of the known that is comfortable, to the new heights of the wonders of God and the invisible realm, which is in fact the place where we all originated from and the place where we are learning to go to up from here.

CHAPTER 8

Living the Dream

The Dream.

I know I have a dream, a misty vision of something much bigger and brighter coming and lifting me up like the eagle soaring above the calamity below and lifting my sight so I can see from the perspective of Heaven and know that Gods Spirit will carry me through and empower my destiny.

To be an effective minister of His love and flow in the gifts, having the nature and character of Christ and being part of a great body of believers working together, complimenting each other and encouraging one another to go higher and see the Kingdom of God reach the great harvest of need and oppression that dominates the world. A non judgmental church that holds out the hand to help the lost and the outcasts of society with the love of the Father, motivating action and healing with the compassion of Jesus.
The church being a place of healing and restoration with love and support for the suffering and the sick.

Is it possible? It is and to some degree it already is happening and growing.

All things are possible and it is OK to dream big things as we have a **BIG GOD** who wants to heal and save the lost. Are we held captive by our past failures and limitations that plague our memories to reach out and go for the desires that are in our hearts?

Psalm 126:1-6
When the LORD brought back the captivity of Zion,
We were like those who dream.
2 Then our mouth was filled with laughter,
And our tongue with singing.
Then they said among the nations,
"The LORD has done great things for them."
3 The LORD has done great things for us,
And we are glad.
4 Bring back our captivity, O LORD,
As the streams in the South.
5 Those who sow in tears
Shall reap in joy.
6 He who continually goes forth weeping,
Bearing seed for sowing,
Shall doubtless come again with rejoicing,
Bringing his sheaves with him.

The time of great reaping in streams of blessing from the bounty of heaven is approaching.

We are entering into a time where our wildest dreams and visions of what we have believed the Kingdom could be like will be made manifest into our earthly realm.

When the unbeliever will no longer wag their tongue in mocking scorn at the ineptitude of the church and how we are powerless and limp compared to the alternative source of black magic that shows off its power in the earth.

I believe there is a coming reformation of the power and ability of the Kingdom of God on earth as it is in Heaven type manifestation, where the church and true believers will move and demonstrate the authority and power of the Kingdom of God motivated by the love of the Father and not have personal agendas for selfish gain.

We can dream the awesome power of God moving in signs and wonders to demonstrate His Glory and usher in a harvest of unbelievers into the Kingdom by His Good News for mankind.

Hebrews 9:8-10
8 the Holy Spirit indicating this, that the way into the Holiest of All was not yet made manifest while the first tabernacle was still standing.
9 It was symbolic for the present time in which both gifts and sacrifices are offered which cannot make him who performed the service perfect in regard to the conscience—
10 concerned only with foods and drinks, various washings, and fleshly ordinances imposed until the time of reformation.

The way into the holiest of all is open to us through the sacrifice of Jesus and it is the Fathers will that we enter in boldly to receive His Grace and know Him more, to take us out of the limitations of fleshly practices to what is a reformation of the church, or Gods sons and daughters on earth, so we can truly be effective in our witness taking a deposit from Heaven into the earth.

Zechariah 4:6-10
6 "This is the word of the Lord to Zerubbabel:
'Not by might nor by power, but by My Spirit,'
Says the Lord of hosts.
7 'Who are you, O great mountain?
Before Zerubbabel you shall become a plain!
And he shall bring forth the capstone
With shouts of "Grace, grace to it!"'"
So he answered and said to me:
8 Moreover the word of the Lord came to me, saying:
9 "The hands of Zerubbabel
Have laid the foundation of this temple;
His hands shall also finish it.
Then you will know
That the Lord of hosts has sent Me to you.
10 For who has despised the day of small things?
For these seven rejoice to see
The plumb line in the hand of Zerubbabel.
They are the eyes of the Lord,
Which scan to and fro throughout the whole earth."

There is an intended might and power by the moving of God's Spirit which is not based on a natural strength of might and power by fleshly practices of men.

This power has the ability to bring down the great mountain of power which limits us from being all that God has promised. Zerubbabel the ruler of the tribe of Judah has laid a foundation of the temple, which represents the church as the holy temple of the priesthood of God.

1 Peter 2:5
5 you also, as living stones, are being built up a spiritual house, a holy priesthood, to offer up spiritual sacrifices acceptable to God through Jesus Christ.
When the capstone is brought forth which is above all, a type of Jesus the King of kings and Lord of lords seated above all authority and the kingdoms of the earth. Zerubbabel being the ruler of the tribe of Judah a direct descendant of King David and Jesus was a descendant from this lineage.

Hebrews 7:14
14 For it is evident that our Lord arose from Judah, of which tribe Moses spoke nothing concerning priesthood.

Jesus is our great High Priest and He is in the likeness of Melchizadek.

Hebrews 7:15-19
15 And it is yet far more evident if, in the likeness of Melchizedek, there arises another priest
16 who has come, not according to the law of a fleshly commandment, but according to the power of an endless life.
17 For He testifies;
"You are a priest forever According to the order of Melchizedek."
18 For on the one hand there is an annulling of the former commandment because of its weakness and unprofitableness,
19 for the law made nothing perfect; on the other hand, there is the bringing in of a better hope, through which we draw near to God.

According to the power of an endless life a priest forever in the order of Melchizadek. You see when the church as His ruling body on earth brings forth the capstone which is placing Jesus as ruling in our lives, then the mountain cannot resist His power and authority and the Spirit of the Lord is free to move according to an endless life and not the law of fleshly commandments, but by the Grace of God, which moves unrestricted by the limitations of the flesh, as we are positioned in the Righteousness of God and have access to the Most Holy Place in the Presence of the Father. No opposing might or power can stop the church from fulfilling its mandate to be Christ in us and His will done on earth as it is heaven from an endless life of abundance of grace to the church.

The Church where Jesus is Lord are ruling and reigning with Christ in the Heavenly Realms far above all other principalities and the dominions of darkness and the effects of iniquity in the hearts of men.

Now with this momentum of the Holy Spirit moving on earth what will happen? The foundation was laid when Jesus died and was resurrected establishing the beginning of Gods Spirit living in His people on earth, this temple will be finished by the hands of Zerubbabel the ruler of the tribe of Judah.

So to sum up the main points we have: -

- *The Foundation laid will; be finished.*
- *Church Foundation – Christ in us.*
- *Early church beginnings of His TEMPLE, His Body the church.*
- *We are a dwelling place for the Holy Spirit*
- *Latter church will finish the building of His temple.*
- *Don't despise the day of small things. Beginnings will always occur as seed of the intentions of God are planted and people are raised up to usher in a wave of Gods Glory.*
- *The Seven rejoice to see the plumbline, why what is the significance?*
- *The Plumbline is like the true word of God, an alignment with the truth of God.*
- *Alignment is a straightening of crooked ways and paths, a True faith and doctrine not tainted by mans philosophy.*

- Hand of Zerubbabel – if we are the Body of Christ then we are His hands on earth.
- The Church in alignment with the Head is a Heart change.
- A repositioning in the Heavenly Realms where Jesus rules.
- The seven eyes of the Lord scan the earth to find hearts that will be true.
- Who is willing and TRUE?
- The Plumbed in.

Ephesians 2:20–22
20 having been built on the foundation of the apostles and prophets, Jesus Christ Himself being the chief cornerstone,
21 in whom the whole building, being fitted together, grows into a holy temple in the Lord,
22 in whom you also are being built together for a dwelling place of God in the Spirit.

NEW and Right, TRUE means plumbline correct.

We see that here are great shouts of victory in the heavenly realms when the Kingdom of God is established on earth and we see Gods Goodness and mercy flow in healing and deliverance and change in peoples hearts towards the things of God and now that is reformation.

Just as there was the early church and then the latter church, the early and latter rains, there comes like two waves or moves of God to begin a work and then finish a work on earth, so we see the shout is Grace, Grace, not just one grace but another grace, like a grace to lay the foundation and then a grace to finish the temple of God. Lets look at this double effect another way – **reformation**.
Like Elijah to come and the double portion anointing, there are many references to a second and final wave that is like the big one to shake the earth.

The early church had the foundation and began the building and Paul the Apostle brought the revelation that would complete the task, however, we know from church history that the early church kind of lost its foundation and what followed was the dark ages. Then we have what is known in Church History as the time of reformation and guess what the foundational teaching was "saved by grace". **Martin Luther** nailed that one literally for the church praise God and he was the monk that turned the world upside down.

Allow me to say this **reformation! reformation!**

What does that mean for the church and where we are at presently?

I believe there will be another grace which is another reformation to finish the temple, it was not completed during the first reformation, it was a time or gaining back what the early church had.

Now the second grace would complete the first *"saved by grace"* with not only **grace to be,** but also **grace to do** the greater works to perform His will on earth.
In Him we do not have any feeble representation, but a reformation of a demonstration of Gods Love and Power in signs and wonders from a clean heart and a new and right spirit that is Christ like.

As He is so are we, walking as He walked, a church that is not by human might or power but by His Spirit in tune with the Head Jesus, the capstone brought forth and above; and the world will know it convincingly and say "the Lord has done great things for them". The Lord has done great things for the church and will do so much more, the world has seen measures and pockets and revivals of His Glory demonstrated.

Under Grace we are no longer under the law that says we are not perfect.
Under Grace we are covered with the righteousness of God.
We act under the Authority of Grace, a position given to us that says we have a right to be living in the newness of life.

Grace is a position that we have in Him and Grace is an ability that we have access to through Him and it is Resurrection Life.

Zechariah 3:4, 5
4 Then He answered and spoke to those who stood before Him, saying, "Take away the filthy garments from him."
And to him He said, "See, I have removed your iniquity from you, and I will clothe you with rich robes."
5 And I said, "Let them put a clean turban on his head."
So they put a clean turban on his head, and they put the clothes on him. And the Angel of the Lord stood by.

What is the sign of reformation? When the filthy robes of the contaminates of this world are removed and a clean turban is in place over our minds.

What are our robes the covering or our glory, what radiates from our hearts, when it is the light of the love of the Father shining forth and the capstone of the Ruling of Jesus is brought forth in our lives, like a turban placed over our thinking by the Mind of Christ.

The temple of God as His body of believers are filled with the Spirit and the Glory of God covering the earth through the church.

Where resurrection life abounds, the abundance of grace is received and permitted to do its work through us, now we are like men who dreamed, that is way beyond what we can conceive, the church functioning as it is described by His word and promises, the plumbline is lining up now with the temple building reaching for completion, Christ is formed in us the Sons and Daughters of God, equipped and empowered of God to do mighty exploits on the earth. We are talking about a latter movement, which will usher in at the appointed time the 2nd Coming of Christ so there it is again the 2nd, a first and then a second, do you see Gods handiwork and pattern written over His plan for mankind and the fulfillment of things on earth.

Now notice the iniquity is removed from Joshua, this is so he can rule unrestricted and have no access from the opposing rule of darkness.

Zechariah 3:8, 9

8 Hear, O Joshua, the high priest,
You and your companions who sit before you,
For they are a wondrous sign;
For behold, I am bringing forth My Servant the BRANCH.
9 For behold, the stone
That I have laid before Joshua:
Upon the stone are seven eyes.
Behold, I will engrave its inscription,'
Says the Lord of hosts,
'And I will remove the iniquity of that land in one day.

Iniquity has been removed effectively in one day on the cross and it is possible that when He returns that this position will be transformed into all of the believers completely or maybe that is the unblemished Bride of Christ?

What is a Wondrous Sign? Believers who walk in authority and rule above where sin does not have dominion and its influence over them.
It is a bringing forth in us, Christ in us.
By the way the verse for *"Christ in us" is Colossians 1:27*
A great mystery now revealed.
My servant the Branch is Jesus our Lord and Saviour.

We abide in Him and He in us, nourished by the life of the branch.
God has measured out His blueprint of destiny in our hearts as believers abiding in the life of God.

Philippians 1:6
6 being confident of this very thing, that He who has begun a good work in you will complete it until the day of Jesus Christ;

We are part of His great plan for mankind and the good work of His design, we are His building of a living entity and His building in us is not an inanimate, concrete block, empire.

Ezekiel 47:1-12
Then he brought me back to the door of the temple; and there was water, flowing from under the threshold of the temple toward the east, for the front of the temple faced east; the water was flowing from under the right side of the temple, south of the altar. 2 He brought me out by way of the north gate, and led me around on the outside to the outer gateway that faces east; and there was water, running out on the right side. 3 And when the man went out to the east with the line in his hand, he measured one thousand cubits,
and he brought me through the waters; the water came up to my ankles.
4 Again he measured one thousand and brought me through the waters; the water came up to my knees. Again he measured one thousand and brought me through; the water came up to my waist.
5 Again he measured one thousand, and it was a river that I could not cross; for the water was too deep, water in which one must swim, a river that could not be crossed. 6 He said to me, "Son of man, have you seen this?" Then he brought me and returned me to the bank of the river.
7 When I returned, there, along the bank of the river, were very many trees on one side and the other.
8 Then he said to me: "This water flows toward the eastern region, goes down into the valley, and enters the sea. When it reaches the sea, its waters are healed.

9 And it shall be that every living thing that moves, wherever the rivers go, will live. There will be a very great multitude of fish, because these waters go there; for they will be healed, and everything will live wherever the river goes.
10 It shall be that fishermen will stand by it from En Gedi to En Eglaim; they will be places for spreading their nets. Their fish will be of the same kinds as the fish of the Great Sea, exceedingly many.
11 But its swamps and marshes will not be healed; they will be given over to salt.
12 Along the bank of the river, on this side and that, will grow all kinds of trees used for food; their leaves will not wither, and their fruit will not fail. They will bear fruit every month, because their water flows from the sanctuary. Their fruit will be for food, and their leaves for medicine."

There is a River of God and it flows from the temple.

There is Healing and Life wherever it goes and when it reaches the seas its waters are healed, the great sea of the masses of mankind need living water to heal what has become polluted. Fishermen of the great commission spread their nets far and wide effectively, with guided and skilled hands and the harvest will be great.

Where this river flows the trees of righteousness will bear fruit, when we abide in Him we produce much fruit, imagine the greater works that Jesus said we would see, you can dream this dream you have His permission.

How can we enter into all that He has for us? Certainly when we are part of His building and we are His temple, we are becoming one with Him and in the likeness of His image and through Him we can do the greater works;

1 John 4:17
⇒ *As He is, so are we in this world.*

Well there is water flowing and it contains life in abundance, not like what the rivers of mankind have become. The Holy Spirit has been poured out for all to be filled with life and we can get into the flow of His life and begin to experience His plan and walk with Him into the deep.

The dream is limitless with an endless life of possibilities and the fruit will be food to the needy and healing to the sick.
His plan to reach mankind is progressive and is building towards a place where there are no limits, ever increasing Glory is being released from His Heavenly temple design which incorporates our earthly temples as we are part of His body, the fullness of Him who fills all in all.

Ephesians 1:22, 23
22 And He put all things under His feet, and gave Him to be head over all things to the church,
23 which is His body, the fullness of Him who fills all in all.

Now you see the intention and the great plan to reach beyond the walls of the temple in an ever increasing glory and river of love bringing healing to the nations.

Ephesians 3:8-12
8 To me, who am less than the least of all the saints, this grace was given, that I should preach among the Gentiles the unsearchable riches of Christ,
9 and to make all see what is the fellowship of the mystery, which from the beginning of the ages has been hidden in God who created all things through Jesus Christ;
10 to the intent that now the manifold wisdom of God might be made known by the church to the principalities and powers in the heavenly places,
11 according to the eternal purpose which He accomplished in Christ Jesus our Lord,
12 in whom we have boldness and access with confidence through faith in Him.

Through His Church, the believers, the intention is to make known the mystery of an outpouring of His grace to be and to do His will on earth.

As a result, the principalities who held mankind in bondage under their throne of iniquity will be devastated and demolished and powerless to stop the very ones who were previously held captive, under their influence and control.

We have access and boldness now to take possession of the authority and delegated ability from the King of kings.

Ezekiel 43:7-12
7 And He said to me, "Son of man, this is the place of My throne and the place of the soles of My feet, where I will dwell in the midst of the children of Israel forever. No more shall the house of Israel defile My holy name, they nor their kings, by their harlotry or with the carcasses of their kings on their high places.
8 When they set their threshold by My threshold, and their doorpost by My doorpost, with a wall between them and Me, they defiled My holy name by the abominations which they committed; therefore I have consumed them in My anger.
9 Now let them put their harlotry and the carcasses of their kings far away from Me, and I will dwell in their midst forever.
10 "Son of man, describe the temple to the house of Israel, that they may be ashamed of their iniquities; and let them measure the pattern.

11 And if they are ashamed of all that they have done, make known to them the design of the temple and its arrangement, its exits and its entrances, its entire design and all its ordinances, all its forms and all its laws. Write it down in their sight, so that they may keep its whole design and all its ordinances, and perform them.
12 This is the law of the temple: The whole area surrounding the mountaintop is most holy. Behold, this is the law of the temple. A place for my Throne

There is a place where we face our iniquities and lifestyle habits that are etched into our memories and behavior patterns. We can give these over to Him as they are already dealt with by the substitution on the cross and the power of His blood.

We give up our lifestyle and shameful ways and take on His pattern and new life by His design, it is imprinted, renewing in our hearts and minds and we live from the bright potential He created us to be. The more we enter in, as now the way is open to us and we have access when we believe; the more the river flows, increasing, miraculously upwards and we will know and experience the mountaintop where He is seated at the right hand of the Father where we are seated with Him.

The whole area we occupy will be holy as He occupies through us; the law is His temple on earth as it is in Heaven. When His glory comes and has free reign things will shift and change, there will be radical change and I believe the greater works will be normal operation in the Body of Believers who enter into this measure. Can you see His pattern? Can you feel His Presence and the desire to change darkness to light and release His Glory to the great needy seas of mankind? Dream with me - you know good dreams originate from above.

Isaiah 60:1-3
Arise, shine;
For your light has come!
And the glory of the Lord is risen upon you.
2 For behold, the darkness shall cover the earth,
And deep darkness the people;
But the Lord will arise over you,
And His glory will be seen upon you.
3 The Gentiles shall come to your light,
And kings to the brightness of your rising.

Remember in this great plan for us, we are all individual and unique in giftings and expression, what does it mean for each of us in a relationship? How I relate to God and interact with Him is not the same as how you enter in, we are all at different places and levels in our walk and we need the now word, the now direction, this comes by practice and getting to know Him, understanding comes for you to follow, expect change and new ways and new places to go in God.

He hasn't changed, we are in the process and God is full of wonder and beauty above description, I think the experience of knowing God and entering into the place of God is way above our imagination, far more than we can ever conceive, forget the rituals and enjoy the journey, it never ends.

I won't choose the same bike as you – colour, shape, size, you know it is variety.
Select the bike to ride that works best for you, just ride on, don't stay off your bike, you will never know what it feels like to ride unless you get on, go on it's the ride of your life, find out what's out there.
The more we have of His Kingdom within, the more we will be able to lead others to glory and a new life, the truth is we will be like stars shining His love in dark places; this world will be changed when God in us comes to town.

Catching the wind of the Spirit.
Like a Yacht putting up sail moving into the right direction and placement.
Comes with experience on the waves of the sea and going through some storms and adversity.
Changes of the weather.
Sensitivity to the seasons and the times.
Beginning is setting out until you know the direction - or the maneuver to take you there.
You are not directing the Spirit you are going with His flow, but if you didn't move then He is not moving apparently.

Our part is getting into position - preparation and launching out when we need to.
Creating the best atmosphere for the sail.
My personal trainer is the Holy Spirit.
Be a Believer who is a Receiver in the right channel – tune into Gods frequency, catch His wave, be in His wind, ride the revolution of His Love and moving of His Spirit.

John 16:13
13 However, when He, the Spirit of truth, has come, He will guide you into all truth; for He will not speak on His own authority, but whatever He hears He will speak; and He will tell you things to come.

The School of the Spirit is the Breakthrough.

Praying in the Spirit builds up your faith, brings revelation of truth and shows you things to come.

Jude 20
20 But you, beloved, building yourselves up on your most holy faith, praying in the Holy Spirit,

Praying in the Spirit is a huge key and a powerful prayer that has the advantage of when our minds do not know what to pray or our minds are struggling to align to Gods ways.

This is Gods secret weapon to bypass the limitations of out thinking and pray the perfect prayer out for our life and destiny, don't neglect this great gift that God has given us to build us up in our faith, we all need building up and strengthening and we can't rely on our mind to work it all out for us.

Enter into the school of the Spirit and His wind will take you higher above the plans of the enemy that keep you down, receive revelation and wisdom in the time of need.
His word is to be taken in, reading, meditating, seeing and gaining insight into truth and security from deception from the word of God.
Worship Him, find the place of rest, be still in His presence, enter in to His courts with praise and go higher up into worship.
Listen, write down, hear what He is saying, see what is the new you, declare your breakthrough, you may dance about it or fast, fast or slow it is your discovery in the wonders and beauty of God who created all.
Find out how He leads you into His endless life, there are so many ways you can surrender your heart to Him.
This word is meant to encourage you and give you revelation on how to go higher. I believe there is so much more to the Kingdom of God and His wonders that the church is yet to enter into, we need to be challenged to go higher in the Kingdom of God, that truly can make a difference in this world that is ruled by darkness.

CHAPTER 9

Grace to Be and to Do

What is Grace?

It's a word that's been tossed around with little respect, misused to get what we want no matter what, but grace and truth delivers a divine ability when understood and applied in real life situations.

Its divine power that you don't naturally have. Its credit put into your account for you to apply to your destiny.

It covers you when you don't measure up and are still learning the ropes, it picks you up when you fall and sets you back on the horse of your course.

Its fail safe, because love never fails, as long as you remain in the vine of the Fathers love and that's pure victory in HIM.

When the only thing we can do is cry for help, because we are just losing it completely, grace is there to reach out to us, it is help in the time of need, it is mercy when the world wants to point the finger.

Amazing Grace nothing compares to its worth, you are best to be in than out, don't be without and left out.

Speak Grace Grace to the mountain.
Not by power not by strength but by My Spirit says the Lord this mountain will be removed.

Love knows no bounds, when sin abounds grace abounds more.
Let me put it simply right here.
Grace is :-
Be Right
AND
Do Call
Grace to Be and to Do.

When all you got is wood hay and stubble, it is time for an upgrade.
Ask for Grace.

God has already written a story about your life, its on His scroll and it is the perfect plan. Anything else will be burnt away and won't hold up against the coming firestorm.
Get on His page it is worth writing about.

Zephaniah 3: 17 The Lord thy God in the midst of thee is mighty; he will save, he will rejoice over thee with joy; he will rest in his love, he will joy over thee with singing.

God gives grace to the humble, He Resists the proud.

God Lifts you up out of the horrible pit.

Ephesians 2:20
We are His workmanship made right in HIM
To do good works to do the greater works in HIM.

As He is so are we in the world.

Being in the Light is someone who has been taken up above the constraints of this world and can rule without hindrance, being able to go up to the place of reigning in this Life from the low places of being under and dictated by circumstances and the systems imposed by this world.

A new state of being – in the light, moving away from striving, resisting, struggling, it is entering into a delight to do His will.
New heart, new behaviour, new pattern of an endless life.

One more defining scripture for grace needs to be included here, this scripture clearly shows grace leads us into developing our character, to take on the very nature of Christ in newness of life.

Titus 2:11,12
11 For the grace of God that bringeth salvation hath appeared to all men,
12 Teaching us that, denying ungodliness and worldly lusts, we should live soberly, righteously, and godly, in this present world;

It is a place of discovery – your uniqueness will be found in the place of exchange and knowing God like never before.

Remember we are part of the Body of Christ and we have a place where we belong. Find the place where you need to be, where growth and the anointing is, fellowship with believers, find powerful visiting ministries, connect with ministries world wide that impart life and take you higher.

If you need help in any area God will direct you to the best place, Pastors, Teachers, Evangelists, Prophets, Apostles and other support ministries are there to equip and build you up. Receive when you need to and give out to others when you are able.

The main thing is that when you have entered into a place in God that lifts you above your circumstances and takes you into your destiny, your Heavenly Father has responded in love, there is faith to move on and breakthrough to the next level.

Revelation 12:11
11 And they overcame him by the blood of the Lamb and by the word of their testimony, and they did not love their lives to the death.

Let's be overcomers in this life by faith in the one true God – the blood of Jesus and let it be our endless overcoming life.

Grace Be Grace Do, the Blood and our Testimony.

Author : Peter Koren
Copyright © August 2012
ISBN 978-1-06706-525-6
www.beinginthelight.com

Grace Be Grace Do 2025 Edition
Is available as

ISBN	Format
978-1-06706-525-6	Grace Be Grace Do PaperBack 2025 Edition
978-1-06706-526-3	Grace Be Grace Do Kindle 2025 Edition
978-1-06706-527-0	Grace Be Grace Do PDF 2025 Edition
978-1-06706-528-7	Grace Be Grace Do EPUB 2025 Edition

I Give Thanks to The King of kings and the Lord of lords - Jesus Christ - the true Author and Finisher of my faith.
He is my Lord and Saviour and friend and I hope yours too.

Transforming Empowering Resurrection Life Scriptures:

Speak out these words of life and inspiration and they will radically change your life :-
• Shift the mountain of opposition.
• Replace lies of the enemy with truth.
• Pour grace on your circumstances and struggles.

Galatians 2:20
I have been crucified with Christ; it is no longer I who live, but Christ lives in me; and the life which I now live in the flesh I live by faith in the Son of God, who loved me and gave Himself for me.

Romans 5:17
For if by the one man's offense death reigned through the one, much more those who receive abundance of grace and of the gift of righteousness will reign in life through the One, Jesus Christ.

Romans 6:4
Therefore we were buried with Him through baptism into death, that just as Christ was raised from the dead by the glory of the Father, even so we also should walk in newness of life.

Romans 6:11
Likewise you also, reckon yourselves to be dead indeed to sin, but alive to God in Christ Jesus our Lord.

Romans 6:14
For sin shall not have dominion over you, for you are not under law but under grace.

Romans 8: 2
For the law of the Spirit of life in Christ Jesus has made me free from the law of sin and death.

Romans 8:11
But if the Spirit of Him who raised Jesus from the dead dwells in you, He who raised Christ from the dead will also give life to your mortal bodies through His Spirit who dwells in you.

2 Timothy 1:7
For God has not given us a spirit of fear, but of power and of love and of a sound mind.

2 Corinthians 5:17
Therefore, if anyone is in Christ, he is a new creation; old things have passed away; behold, all things have become new.

2 Peter 1:2-4
2 Grace and peace be multiplied to you in the knowledge of God and of Jesus our Lord, 3 as His divine power has given to us all things that pertain to life and godliness, through the knowledge of Him who called us by glory and virtue,

4 by which have been given to us exceedingly great and precious promises, that through these you may be partakers of the divine nature, having escaped the corruption that is in the world through lust.

2 Peter 1:19
And so we have the prophetic word confirmed, which you do well to heed as a light that shines in a dark place, until the day dawns and the morning star rises in your hearts;

Zechariah 4:6
This is the word of the Lord to Zerubbabel: 'Not by might nor by power, but by My Spirit,' Says the Lord of hosts.

Zechariah 4:7
Who are you, O great mountain? Before Zerubbabel you shall become a plain! And he shall bring forth the capstone With shouts of
"Grace, Grace to it!"

Revelation 12:11
And they overcame him by the blood of the Lamb and by the word of their testimony, and they did not love their lives to the death.

Unless otherwise indicated, Bible quotations are taken from New King James Version of the Bible. Copyright © 1982 by Thomas Nelson, Inc. Used by permission. All rights reserved.

Iniquity: *Meaning of this word according to what I have learnt is crookedness, perversion, twisted behaviour or addictions, an ingrained sin that becomes like impulse in a situation and it appears this can be Generational, handed down and becoming part of an identity. That's why it is a miracle when we are set free from iniquity.*

Grace Be Grace Do images attribution:-

Cover Art

Knight
"iStock.com/Guillermo Perales Gonzale"
Used as Reference for Original Painting and B&W Arrangement. Art Work and changes made by Peter Koren

Vector Flourish Ornaments
All Silhouettes put together a massive floral set of free flourish ornaments made with clean and clear vector lines.
Creative Commons
Attribution-ShareAlike 3.0 Unported (CC BY-SA 3.0)

2D Square in 3D Sphere
Peter Koren Design

Other Books by this Author:

Older Brother the Other

Walk the Talk on Hot Coals

Seeing Beyond 2020 Vision

www.ingramcontent.com/pod-product-compliance
Lightning Source LLC
Chambersburg PA
CBHW010448010526
44118CB00019B/2510